SOUPS & CHOWDERS

SOUPS & CHOWDERS
FROM THE BLENDER TO THE BOWL

This edition published in 2012
LOVE FOOD is an imprint of Parragon Books Ltd

Parragon
Queen Street House
4 Queen Street
Bath BA1 1HE, UK

Copyright © Parragon Books Ltd 2010

LOVE FOOD and the accompanying heart device is a registered trade mark of Parragon Books Ltd in
Australia, the UK, USA, India and the EU.

www.parragon.com/lovefood

ISBN: 978-1-4454-8911-7

Printed in China

Introduction by Christine McFadden

Notes for the Reader

This book uses both metric and imperial measurements. Follow the same units of measurement
throughout; do not mix metric and imperial. All spoon measurements are level: teaspoons are assumed
to be 5 ml, and tablespoons are assumed to be 15 ml. Unless otherwise stated, milk is assumed to be
full fat, eggs and individual vegetables are medium, and pepper is freshly ground black pepper. Unless
otherwise stated, all root vegetables should be washed and peeled prior to using.

Garnishes, decorations and serving suggestions are all optional and not necessarily included in the recipe
ingredients or method.

The times given are an approximate guide only. Preparation times differ according to the techniques used
by different people and the cooking times may also vary from those given. Optional ingredients, variations
or serving suggestions have not been included in the time calculations.

Recipes using raw or very lightly cooked eggs should be avoided by infants, the elderly, pregnant women,
convalescents and anyone suffering from an illness. Pregnant and breastfeeding women are advised to
avoid eating peanuts and peanut products. Sufferers from nut allergies should be aware that some of the
ready-made ingredients used in the recipes in this book may contain nuts. Always check the packaging
before use.

Picture acknowledgements

The publisher would like to thank Getty Images following for permission to reproduce copyright material
on the following pages: 164–165

Contents

Introduction

Taking a cook's look around the world, there is hardly a country that doesn't have its favourite soup – from American chowders and Russian borscht to Spanish gazpacho and Scotch broth, and many more. This popularity is hardly surprising. Soups are comforting, appetizing, nutritious, and as easy on the pocket as on the waistline. They put to good use morsels of meat or fish, leftover rice and pasta, and vegetables that are slightly past their best. They simmer happily on the stove, leaving you free to relax or get on with other things. The ultimate in convenience, soups can be prepared in advance, then chilled or frozen, ready to reheat when needed. Soups are wonderfully adaptable – warming in winter and refreshing in summer, a well-made soup gives you a feeling of well-being, is satisfying but also easy to digest, and is as suitable for a solitary supper as for feeding a crowd.

Essential Ingredients for Soup-making

STORECUPBOARD INGREDIENTS

An impressive range of soups can be made from storecupboard ingredients. If you enjoy making soup and want to do so regularly, it's worth stocking up on the basics. Storecupboard items usually have a long shelf life, but make sure you check the 'use-by' dates regularly and discard any that are out of date.

Stock

Good-quality stock is the foundation of all good soups. Home-made stock has the best flavour, but shop-bought stock is a useful fallback. Jellied or concentrated liquid stock is generally a good choice. Stock cubes vary in quality and tend to be over-salty.

Oils

Flavourless vegetable oils, such as sunflower, grapeseed or rapeseed oil, are used for the preliminary softening of vegetables. Oils with a strong flavour, such as extra virgin olive oil or toasted sesame oil, are best reserved for a final drizzle before serving the soup. Store oils in a dark cupboard away from heat.

Pasta and noodles

Thin dried pasta and small shapes are essential for minestrone and other hearty mixed soups. Asian noodles add bulk and texture to clear soups. Cook them before adding to soup.

Grains

Rice, pearl barley and spelt are satisfying additions to all kinds of soups. Naturally bland, they team well with robustly flavoured vegetables and potent aromatics.

Pulses

Pulses include dried beans, lentils and chickpeas. With their soft creamy texture and earthy flavours they make some of the best-tasting soups. With the exception of lentils, dried pulses need lengthy soaking and cooking before adding to soup. Canned pulses are a convenient alternative as they do not need any pre-cooking or soaking.

Salt

Salt is a must for soups – even a small amount will improve the flavour. Use free-flowing table salt for seasoning soup as it cooks. Sprinkle with a few sea salt flakes just before serving to provide crunchy texture and bursts of flavour.

Seasonings, sauces and condiments

Sold in handy bottles and jars, these have a long shelf life. A teaspoon of soy sauce will round out an Asian-style soup, as will a few drops of Thai fish sauce. Worcestershire sauce adds savoury piquancy. Tabasco sauce has a powerful fiery kick. Tubes of tomato purée and anchovy paste are useful flavour boosters too.

Spices

Spices add exciting flavours and fragrance to soups. The most useful are black pepper, chilli flakes, cayenne pepper, paprika, cumin, and coriander seeds. Nutmeg and cinnamon also come in handy. Spices quickly lose their potency once ground so buy them whole and grind as needed. Store in airtight containers in a cool, dark cupboard.

Dried herbs

Robust herbs, such as rosemary, oregano, sage and thyme, keep their flavour when dried. Add to vegetables before adding stock, so that they have time to release their flavours during the preliminary frying. Buy in small quantities and store in airtight containers in a dark cupboard away from heat.

Dried mushrooms

Morels, shiitake and porcini have an exceptionally meaty flavour when dried. Soak in hot water for about 15 minutes before using. The drained soaking liquid can be added to stock.

Thickening agents

Flour-based thickeners bind liquids and solids in soups, holding the solids in suspension. To thicken 1 litre/1¾ pints, sizzle 25 g/1 oz wheat flour with an equal weight of butter, stirring until smooth, before gradually whisking in the liquid. Bring to the boil, then simmer for at least 5 minutes, stirring constantly.

Cornflour, arrowroot and potato flour are useful for thickening clear soups. They are quick to cook and produce a slightly glutinous texture. Mix to a thin paste with water before adding to hot liquid. Add towards the end of cooking, stirring well while thickening.

Rice flour is another option. It can be safely sprinkled directly into hot liquid, without forming unwanted lumps.

Vinegar

A few drops of wine vinegar or rice vinegar will sharpen the flavour of most soups. Balsamic vinegar is sweeter and syrupy, and is best used for drizzling on soup just before serving.

FRESH INGREDIENTS

A well-stocked refrigerator or larder will not only provide the essentials for soup and stock, it will also help you create tasty garnishes and make the most of fresh produce as it comes into season.

Dairy products

Dairy products add richness and body to soups. They also provide valuable nutrients, such as protein and calcium.

Butter may be used for the preliminary softening of vegetables or swirled in at the end of cooking to round out the flavour.

Cheese is used mainly as a garnish. Hard cheeses, such as Parmesan and Cheddar, are useful for grating. Melting cheeses, such as mozzarella and Gruyère, make tasty toppings for croûtes (see page 13). Crumbled feta adds a salty tang.

Cream, soured cream and crème fraîche add rich flavours and silky texture. Do not add them to boiling soup, as they may curdle (see page 13 for advice on rescuing a curdled soup).

Natural yogurt cuts the flavour of rich soups or it can be used in its own right as a base for chilled soups. Avoid adding yogurt to boiling soup, as it will curdle.

Fish and seafood

Fish and seafood have subtle flavours and a delicate texture. They need gentle cooking to prevent them from disintegrating or becoming tough.

Monkfish, halibut and snapper fillets are the basis for mixed fish soups, such as bouillabaisse. Cut into large chunks and cook gently until opaque.

Salmon is good in light soups, either with young spring vegetables or thin noodles. Use chunks cut from meaty cutlets, or strips from the tail end where there are fewer bones.

Prawns, fresh or frozen, are indispensable for Asian-style clear soups or creamy laksas. You may prefer to devein prawns before you use them – that is, to remove the black line (the intestinal tract) running along the back of each prawn. Cook prawns quickly until opaque. Do not overcook or they will become tough.

Clams are a traditional ingredient in creamy chowders. Scrub and rinse well before using.

Meat

Meat makes nourishing soups with deeply satisfying flavours. A little goes a long way and cheaper cuts become meltingly tender after leisurely simmering. Leftover cooked meat can also be used in soups.

Beef and lamb provide substantial flavours that stand up to potent spices, cabbage and other strongly flavoured vegetables. For slow-cooked soups, use cheaper cuts, such as beef flank or shoulder of lamb. Cut into bite-sized chunks, removing any visible fat and gristle. Minced beef or lamb make flavoursome miniature meatballs to bulk out soups.

Pork has a distinctive slightly sweet flavour that is equally good with creamy soups or spicy oriental soups. Use fillet or boneless chops, cut into thin strips or small cubes. Bacon is a useful ingredient for adding flavour to all kinds of soup.

Poultry

There are literally hundreds of poultry soups. They are universally popular and among the most comforting.

Chicken and turkey can be used more or less interchangeably. Cut the meat into thin strips or bite-sized cubes, discarding the skin. The meat from thighs and drumsticks is more succulent than breast meat and has more flavour.

Duck produces flavoursome juices and is particularly good in Asian-style soups. Its characteristic sweetness goes well with spices, such as star anise and fennel. Cut the meat into thin strips or bite-sized cubes, taking care to remove the skin and fat.

Vegetables

The sheer versatility of vegetables makes them the basis for countless inspiring soups. They offer appetizing flavours, textures and colours, and are a rich source of health-promoting vitamins and minerals.

Basics

Celery, carrots and onions are essential for stock-making. Together they create a complex flavour that is the foundation for all good soups.

Potatoes, parsnips and celeriac provide body and earthy sweetness. Floury potatoes can be mashed and used as a thickener.

Garlic, shallots and leeks add mellow sweet flavours. They become meltingly soft as they cook down.

Leafy greens, such as spinach, cabbage and chard, provide colour, potent flavour and vital vitamins. They are especially good added to meaty soups or those based on beans and pasta. Remove and discard tough stalks and slice the leaves into ribbons before adding to soup. Spinach and chard produce plenty of extra liquid, so you may need less stock.

Seasonal vegetables

Asparagus, young peas, courgettes and sweetcorn make deliciously fresh-tasting summery soups. Use them within 24 hours of picking or buying, while the flavours are at their best.

Rocket and watercress make vibrant peppery soups. Add potato or cream to give the soup body.

Tomatoes and peppers are at their best in mid-to-late summer. They are delicious in chilled gazpacho and other Mediterranean-style soups.

Pumpkins and butternut squash make colourful autumn soups. Cut into wedges and roast them to boost the flavour, then blend to a rich velvety purée.

Jerusalem artichokes have a unique nutty flavour. Cook them in milk and stock for a fortifying winter soup.

Mushrooms lend a sweet earthy taste to all kinds of soups. They are perfect for adding body and flavour to meat soups and are a great addition to Asian-style soups. To clean, wipe mushrooms with damp kitchen paper – do not immerse them in water.

Puréeing Soups

Some soups need to be puréed to make them smoother or more palatable. Exceptions are clear soups, such as chicken noodle soup, and chunky soups, such as minestrone. There are also semi-puréed soups in which only about half to two thirds of the soup is puréed. The resulting liquid is then combined with the reserved solid ingredients, which give the soup an interesting texture as well as an indication of what went into it.

Your choice of utensil will depend on the amount to be puréed, how smooth you want the soup to be, and whether you prefer the speed of an electrically-powered machine or are happy to do the job by hand.

Blender
For a really silky-smooth soup, it's best to use a blender. The blades whirl at a higher speed than a food processor, producing a finer textured purée. The narrow goblet keeps solid ingredients within reach of the blades, so you don't have to keep stopping and stirring. It's a good idea to hold down the lid with a folded cloth, as the contents can rise up and overflow when the blades start to rotate, especially if the soup is still hot. To prevent mishaps, it's best not to fill the goblet past the halfway point.

Food processor
The bowl of a food processor can cope with larger quantities than a blender. The pulse button makes it easy to control the texture, although the end result will not be as smooth as soup from a blender because the wider base means that less of the soup comes into contact with the blades.

Stick blender
Handy for puréeing soup in a saucepan, the stick blender has a short horizontal blade at the end of a rotating metal stick. As you move it round the pan, it breaks down solids, producing a reasonably smooth purée. The real bonus of using a stick blender is that it is much easier to clean than other utensils – the blade end is usually detachable and simply needs to be rinsed under running water.

Food mill/moulis-légumes
One of the most useful non-electric gadgets, the food mill resembles a colander with folding feet that clamp over a bowl to hold it steady. It is fitted with a spring-mounted handle that clips over a perforated metal disc. As you rotate the handle, the food is pushed through the disc and the resulting purée drops into the bowl below.

Conical sieve/chinois
Also called a 'bouillon strainer', this deep cone-shaped sieve is ideal for producing very smooth purées by hand. The ultra-fine mesh clears stocks of every trace of sediment and strains softened vegetables to a velvety purée. It comes with a tapered wooden pestle that fits into the base of the cone, and presses the last drop of liquid from solid ingredients.

Garnishes & Serving Suggestions

GARNISHES

Attractive garnishes sharpen the appetite and reflect the character of the soup. When choosing garnishes, aim for contrasting colour and texture, and a flavour that complements the soup.

Herbs

A sprinkling of fresh green herbs will bring any soup to life. Choose tender-leaved varieties, chop them roughly and add at the last minute.

Spices

Zesty spices, such as black peppercorns, cumin or coriander seeds, add potent flavour to vegetable or pulse-based soups. Grind them freshly and add just before serving. Add a pinch of crushed chilli flakes or paprika for vibrant colour.

Pesto and tapenade (black olive paste)

A slick of pesto will add sharpness and brilliant colour to pasta or bean soups. Inky tapenade goes particularly well with tomato or red pepper soups.

Oils

Trickled over soup just before serving, extra virgin olive oil adds richness, colour and smoothness. Toasted sesame oil is good with Oriental-style soups.

Nuts and seeds

Chopped toasted nuts add flavour and crunch to puréed vegetable soups. Pumpkin, sunflower and sesame seeds also add texture and colour.

Bacon

Snippets of crisp-fried streaky bacon add flavour, colour and texture to pale puréed soups.

Vegetables

Sizzled wisps of carrot, parsnip or leek make a stunning garnish to puréed or cream soups. Chopped spring onion tops or deseeded diced tomato add vibrant colour.

Cream and yogurt

A swirl of cream or yogurt adds richness to mild-flavoured soups and tames the heat of spicy soups. To prevent curdling, never add to boiling soup but add it off the heat, just before serving. Double cream and crème fraîche have a high fat content and are less likely to curdle than lower-fat varieties, such as soured cream or single cream. Thick Greek-style yogurt is less likely to curdle than ordinary yogurt.

Aïoli (see page 168)

A rich garlicky mayonnaise, delicious with Mediterranean fish or vegetable soups.

Rouille (see page 167)

A powerful red garlicky sauce from Provence, traditionally served with bouillabaisse and other fish soups. Spread it on croûtes or swirl directly into the soup.

SERVING SUGGESTIONS

Soup can sometimes leave you feeling temporarily full but not necessarily satisfied. A tasty accompaniment will transform this light meal into something more hearty and substantial.

Breads

Bread is the perfect partner to a bowl of steaming soup. It adds bulk and also allows you to mop up every last drop from the bowl. Nowadays, there is a wonderful choice available from bakeries and supermarkets, ranging from the traditional farmhouse loaf to speciality breads from all over the world. If you fancy trying your hand at making your own breads, you will find plenty of tasty recipes in Chapter 6 of this book (see pages 202–221).

Ciabatta is an Italian slipper-shaped bread with an open texture and crisp crust. Good with minestrone or tomato-based soups.

Flatbreads are yeast-free breads that include chewy naan bread, chapattis, pitta bread, tortillas and wraps. Use them to wipe out the soup bowl or break into small pieces and stir into the soup for added bulk.

Focaccia is a salty Italian flattened bread with a dimpled surface, sometimes topped with rosemary or onion. Excellent for mopping up Italian soups.

Garlic bread is made from Italian or French bread that has been spread with garlic butter and heated in the oven. Good with Mediterranean-style soups.

Sourdough is a traditional slow-fermented loaf with a slightly tangy flavour. Goes well with most soups.

Croûtons (see page 205)

Cubes of day-old bread, fried until golden and crisp. Good for adding contrasting crunch to smooth creamy soups.

Croûtes

Thick slices of oven-dried French bread served plain or garnished with various toppings. Useful for padding out thinnish soups. To make plain croûtes, slice a thin day-old baguette and arrange on a baking sheet. Bake in a preheated oven at 180°C/350°F/Gas Mark 4, turning once, for about 5 minutes, until golden and crisp.

To make cheese croûtes, bake the baguette slices for 1–2 minutes, until just crisp. Brush one side with melted butter and top with grated cheese or a slice of goat's cheese. Return to the oven and bake until the cheese has melted.

TROUBLESHOOTING

When you're new to soup-making, or even if you've been doing it a while, there are a few common problems that occasionally crop up.

• The soup is too thick: dilute with extra stock or other liquid, depending on the type of soup. Reheat thoroughly and adjust the seasoning as necessary.

• The soup is too thin: try adding cooked mashed potato or another starchy vegetable. Alternatively, thicken with breadcrumbs, finely ground nuts, or flour (see pages 8–9). Make sure the flour is thoroughly cooked either before or after it goes in the soup.

• Puréed soup is lumpy: process again briefly in a blender. Take care not to over-process; potatoes can become gluey. Alternatively, push the purée through a sieve.

• The soup is too salty: add 2 peeled potatoes, simmer for 15 minutes, then remove them. The potatoes will absorb some of the salt. Alternatively, try adding extra liquid, such as milk, cream or salt-free stock. This will increase the proportion of liquid to salt and reduce the salty taste.

• The soup is too bland: add a few drops of vinegar or lemon juice to brighten the flavour.

• Cream or yogurt has curdled: the soup was too hot when the cream was added. You may be able to rescue it by combining 1 tablespoon of cornflour with 1½ tablespoons of water for every 500 ml/18 fl oz of soup. Mix to a smooth paste, stir in a cupful of soup, then whisk the mixture into the remaining soup. Heat gently for 5 minutes, stirring, to cook the cornflour. Process in batches in a blender, then push through a fine sieve before reheating gently. The flavour will be blander so you may need to add more salt.

Making Fresh Stock

Home-made stock will lift an otherwise ordinary soup, giving it rich, satisfying flavour. The basic method is always the same: the ingredients are simmered very gently in water until all the flavour is extracted. The exact time depends on the type of stock: vegetable stock takes about 30 minutes whilst brown stock needs 2–3 hours.

Tips
• Always start off with cold water. If you try to speed up the process with hot water, you will end up with murky stock.

• Add enough cold water to cover the ingredients by no more than 5 cm/2 inches.

• Bring stock to the boil slowly. This allows foam to collect on the surface where it can be easily skimmed off.

• Never let stock boil for more than a few minutes, or you will end up with muddy liquid.

• Unless specified in the stock recipe, do not add salt. The flavour intensifies as the stock reduces and may become overpowering. Add it when you make the soup.

• Remove the layer of fat before using stock. It will solidify once chilled and be easy to lift off.

Storing stock
• Do not leave stock to cool in the stockpot. It must be cooled quickly and stored in the refrigerator without delay.

• Decant into smaller containers to speed up cooling.

• Once completely cold, store in sealed plastic boxes in the refrigerator for 4–5 days, or in the freezer for 4–6 months.

ESSENTIAL EQUIPMENT

Stockpot
The tall, narrow shape keeps evaporation to a minimum, which in turn means that the contents remain submerged in liquid. The most useful size is 10 litres/17½ pints – remember it can always double up as a pasta pot.

Perforated skimmer
The extra-wide flat bowl scoops up foam that rises to the surface as the stock heats.

Colander
Use for straining bones and vegetables. Make sure it has a sturdy lip or ear-shaped handles for resting on a saucepan or bowl.

Muslin
Use for a second straining to filter out fat and sediment. Arrange a double thickness of damp muslin in a sieve set over a bowl, then pour in previously strained stock.

Brown Stock
Makes about 1.2 litres/2 pints

900 g/2 lb meat bones, raw or cooked
1 large onion
1 large carrot
2 celery sticks
1 bouquet garni*
1.7 litres/3 pints water

1 Preheat the oven to 200°C/400°F/ Gas Mark 6. Place the bones in a roasting tin and cook in the preheated oven for 20 minutes, or until browned. Remove from the oven and leave to cool.
2 Meanwhile, cut the onion, carrots and celery into large dice and set aside.
3 Chop the bones into small pieces and place in a large saucepan with the vegetables and bouquet garni. Pour in the water and slowly bring to the boil, skimming off any foam that rises to the surface. Reduce the heat, cover and simmer for 2 hours.
4 Strain the stock into a bowl and leave to cool. Cover and store in the refrigerator. When cold, remove and discard the layer of fat from the surface.

* For a fresh bouquet garni, place 1 piece of celery, 1–2 small pieces of celery stalk, 2–3 cloves, 1 bay leaf, a few black peppercorns, 2–3 fresh parsley sprigs and 1 fresh thyme sprig in the centre of a small piece of muslin, then tie up with a long length of kitchen string, which can then be tied to the pan handle for easy removal.

Chicken Stock
Makes about 2.5 litres/4½ pints

1 chicken, weighing about 1 kg/2 lb 4 oz
3 carrots
5 shallots
1 onion
1 leek
2 celery sticks
1 garlic bulb
4 litres/7 pints water
1 fresh rosemary sprig
1 fresh thyme sprig
2 bay leaves
1 tsp white peppercorns
5 cloves
3 fresh parsley sprigs

1 Cut the chicken into large pieces. Cut the carrots, shallots, onion, leek and celery into large chunks. Cut the garlic bulb in half horizontally.
2 Pour the water into a large saucepan and add the chicken. Slowly bring to the boil, skimming off any foam that rises to the surface. Add the vegetables, garlic, rosemary, thyme, bay leaves, peppercorns and cloves, and simmer, occasionally skimming off the foam from the surface, for about 45 minutes.
3 Just before the stock is cooked, add the parsley and remove from the heat.
4 Remove the chicken pieces and set aside for later use. Strain the stock into a bowl and leave to cool. Cover and store in the refrigerator. When cold, remove and discard the layer of fat from the surface.

Vegetable Stock
Makes about 2.2 litres/3¾ pints

½ fennel bulb
1 leek
3 carrots
2 celery sticks
2 onions
1 tomato
1 garlic bulb
2.5 litres/4½ pints water
1 fresh rosemary sprig
1 bay leaf
1 tsp white peppercorns
½ tsp fennel seeds

1 Remove any brown spots from the fennel and cut into large dice.
2 Cut the leek, carrots, celery and onions into large dice. Cut the tomato and garlic bulb in half horizontally.
3 Pour the water into a large saucepan and add all the vegetables. Add the garlic, rosemary, bay leaf, peppercorns and fennel seeds, slowly bring to the boil and simmer for about 20 minutes.
4 Strain the stock into a bowl and leave to cool. Cover and store in the refrigerator.

Fish Stock
Makes about 2.5 litres/4½ pints

1 kg/2 lb 4 oz white fish heads, bones and trimmings, rinsed
1 onion
3 shallots
½ fennel bulb
3 celery sticks
1 garlic bulb
3 tbsp vegetable oil
10 white peppercorns
½ tsp fennel seeds
20 g/⅔ oz sea salt
2 bay leaves
250 ml/9 fl oz white wine
50 ml/2 fl oz dry vermouth
1.5 litres/2¾ pints water
2 lemon slices
1 fresh basil sprig
1 fresh thyme sprig

1 Cut out and discard the gills from any fish heads, then soak the fish heads, bones and trimmings for 30 minutes.
2 Cut the onion, shallots, fennel and celery into medium dice. Cut the garlic bulb in half horizontally.
3 Heat the oil in a large saucepan, add the vegetables and cook for 5 minutes, until softened but not browned. Add the garlic, peppercorns, fennel seeds, sea salt and bay leaves.
4 Drain the fish well, then add to the pan and sweat briefly. Add the wine, vermouth and water and slowly bring to a simmer, skimming off any foam that rises to the surface.
5 Simmer gently, occasionally skimming off the foam from the surface, for about 15 minutes. Add the lemon slices, basil and thyme and simmer for a further 5 minutes.
6 Strain the stock into a bowl and leave to cool. Cover and store in the refrigerator.

Chapter 1
Summer Vegetable Soups

Creamy Tomato
& Basil Soup

Serves 6

ingredients

- 25 g/1 oz butter
- 1 tbsp olive oil
- 1 onion, finely chopped
- 1 garlic clove, chopped
- 900 g/2 lb plum tomatoes, chopped
- 700 ml/1¼ pints vegetable stock
- 125 ml/4 fl oz dry white wine
- 2 tbsp sun-dried tomato paste
- 2 tbsp torn fresh basil leaves, plus extra whole leaves to garnish
- 150 ml/5 fl oz double cream
- salt and pepper

1 Melt the butter with the oil in a large heavy-based saucepan. Add the onion and cook, stirring occasionally, for 5 minutes, or until softened. Add the garlic, tomatoes, stock, wine and sun-dried tomato paste, stir well and season to taste with salt and pepper. Partially cover the saucepan and simmer, stirring occasionally, for 20–25 minutes, or until the mixture is soft and pulpy.

2 Remove the saucepan from the heat and leave to cool slightly. Transfer to a food processor or blender, in batches if necessary, add the torn basil and process to a purée. Push the mixture through a sieve into the rinsed-out pan.

3 Stir the cream into the soup and reheat gently, but do not let it boil. Ladle the soup into warmed bowls, garnish with whole basil leaves and serve immediately.

Minestrone

Serves 6

ingredients

- 2 tbsp olive oil
- 1 Spanish onion, chopped
- 2 garlic cloves, finely chopped
- 2 celery sticks, chopped
- ½ small white cabbage,
  cored and shredded
- 150 ml/5 fl oz red wine
- 1.7 litres/3 pints vegetable stock
- 55 g/2 oz dried cannellini beans,
  soaked overnight and drained
- 4 plum tomatoes, peeled,
  deseeded and chopped
- 2 tbsp tomato purée
- 2 tsp sugar
- 2 carrots, diced
- 55 g/2 oz fresh shelled peas
- 55 g/2 oz French beans,
  cut into short lengths
- 55 g/2 oz dried soup pasta
- 2 tbsp chopped fresh mixed
  herbs
- salt and pepper
- freshly grated Parmesan cheese,
  to serve

1 Heat the oil in a large saucepan. Add the onion, garlic and celery and cook over a low heat, stirring occasionally, for 5–7 minutes, until the onion has softened. Stir in the cabbage and cook, stirring frequently, for a further 5 minutes.

2 Increase the heat to medium, pour in the wine and cook for about 2 minutes, until the alcohol has evaporated, then pour in the stock. Add the cannellini beans and bring to the boil, then reduce the heat, cover and simmer for 2½ hours.

3 Add the tomatoes, tomato purée, sugar, carrots, peas, French beans, pasta and herbs and season to taste with salt and pepper. Simmer for 20–25 minutes, until the pasta is cooked and the vegetables are tender.

4 Ladle the soup into warmed bowls and serve immediately with Parmesan cheese.

Carrot & Coriander Soup

Serves 6

ingredients
- 3 tbsp olive oil
- 1 red onion, chopped
- 1 large potato, chopped
- 1 celery stick, chopped
- 500 g/1 lb 2 oz carrots, chopped
- 1 litre/1¾ pints vegetable stock
- 15 g/½ oz butter
- 2 tsp coriander seeds, crushed, plus extra to garnish
- 1½ tbsp chopped fresh coriander, plus extra to garnish
- 225 ml/8 fl oz milk
- salt and pepper

1 Heat the oil in a large saucepan. Add the onion and cook over a low heat, stirring occasionally, for 5 minutes, until softened.

2 Add the potato and celery and cook, stirring occasionally, for 5 minutes, then add the carrots and cook, stirring occasionally, for a further 5 minutes. Cover the pan, reduce the heat to very low and cook, shaking the pan occasionally, for 10 minutes.

3 Pour in the stock and bring to the boil, then cover and simmer for 10 minutes, until the vegetables are tender.

4 Meanwhile, melt the butter in a frying pan. Add the coriander seeds and cook, stirring constantly, for 1 minute. Add the chopped coriander and cook, stirring constantly, for 1 minute, then remove from the heat.

5 Remove the soup from the heat and leave to cool slightly. Transfer to a food processor or blender, in batches if necessary, and process to a purée. Return the soup to the rinsed-out pan, stir in the coriander mixture and milk, and season to taste with salt and pepper. Reheat gently until warmed through. Ladle into warmed bowls, garnish with crushed coriander seeds and chopped coriander and serve immediately.

Roasted Vegetable Soup

Serves 6

ingredients
- 2 aubergines
- 4 tomatoes
- 2 red peppers
- 2 onions, unpeeled
- 2 garlic cloves, unpeeled
- 4 tbsp olive oil
- 1 fresh oregano sprig
- 1.5 litres/2¾ pints chicken or vegetable stock
- salt and pepper
- chopped fresh basil, to garnish

1 Preheat the oven to 180°C/350°F/ Gas Mark 4. Prick the aubergines several times with a fork and put in a roasting tin. Add the tomatoes, peppers and unpeeled onions and garlic. Sprinkle with 2 tablespoons of the oil. Roast in the preheated oven for 30 minutes, then remove the tomatoes. Roast the aubergines, peppers, onions and garlic for a further 30 minutes, until very soft and the pepper skins have blackened.

2 Put the cooked roasted vegetables in a bowl, cover with a damp tea towel and leave for 3–4 hours or overnight, until cold. When cold, cut the aubergines in half, scoop out the flesh and put in the bowl. Remove the skin from the tomatoes, cut in half and discard the seeds and add the flesh to the bowl. Hold the peppers over the bowl to collect the juices and peel off the skin. Remove the stem, core and seeds and add the flesh to the bowl. Peel the onions, cut into quarters and add to the bowl. Squeeze the garlic cloves out of their skin into the bowl.

3 Heat the remaining oil in a large saucepan. Add the vegetables and their juices, the leaves from the oregano sprig, and salt and pepper to taste, then cook gently, stirring frequently, for about 30 minutes. Add the stock and bring to the boil, then simmer for 30 minutes.

4 Remove the saucepan from the heat and leave to cool slightly. Transfer to a food processor or blender, in batches if necessary, and process to a purée. Return the soup to the rinsed-out pan and reheat gently. Ladle into warmed bowls, garnish with basil and serve immediately.

Curried Courgette Soup

Serves 4

ingredients
- 10 g/¼ oz butter
- 1 large onion, finely chopped
- 900 g/2 lb courgettes, sliced
- 450 ml/16 fl oz vegetable stock
- 1 tsp curry powder
- 125 ml/4 fl oz soured cream, plus extra to serve
- salt and pepper

1 Melt the butter in a large saucepan over a medium heat. Add the onion and cook for about 3 minutes, until beginning to soften.

2 Add the courgettes, stock and curry powder, then season to taste with salt. Bring the soup to the boil, then reduce the heat, cover and cook gently for about 25 minutes, until the vegetables are tender.

3 Remove the saucepan from the heat and leave to cool slightly. Transfer to a food processor or blender, in batches if necessary, and process to a purée.

4 Return the soup to the rinsed-out pan, stir in the soured cream and reheat gently, but do not let it boil.

5 Taste and adjust the seasoning, adding salt and pepper if needed. Ladle into warmed bowls, top each with a spoonful of soured cream and serve immediately.

Watercress Soup

Serves 4

ingredients
- 2 bunches of watercress, about 200 g/7 oz
- 40 g/1½ oz butter
- 2 onions, chopped
- 225 g/8 oz potatoes, roughly chopped
- 1.2 litres/2 pints vegetable stock or water
- freshly grated nutmeg (optional)
- salt and pepper
- 125 ml/4 fl oz crème fraîche, to serve

1 Remove the leaves from the watercress and set aside. Roughly chop the stalks.

2 Melt the butter in a large saucepan over a medium heat, add the onions and cook for 4–5 minutes, until soft. Do not brown.

3 Add the potatoes to the saucepan and mix well with the onions. Add the watercress stalks and the stock.

4 Bring to the boil, then reduce the heat, cover and simmer for 15–20 minutes, until the potatoes are soft.

5 Add the watercress leaves and stir in gently. Remove the saucepan from the heat and leave to cool slightly. Transfer to a food processor or blender, in batches if necessary, and process to a purée. Return the soup to the rinsed-out pan and reheat gently. Season to taste with salt, pepper and nutmeg, if using.

6 Ladle into warmed bowls and top each with a spoonful of crème fraîche and a grating of nutmeg, if using. Serve immediately.

Lettuce & Rocket Soup

Serves 4–6

ingredients
- 15 g/½ oz butter
- 1 large onion, halved and sliced
- 2 leeks, sliced
- 1.5 litres/2¾ pints vegetable stock
- 85 g/3 oz white rice
- 2 carrots, thinly sliced
- 3 garlic cloves
- 1 bay leaf
- 2 heads of soft round lettuce (about 450 g/1 lb), cored and chopped
- 175 ml/6 fl oz double cream
- freshly grated nutmeg
- 85 g/3 oz rocket leaves, finely chopped, plus extra leaves to garnish
- salt and pepper
- crusty bread, to serve

1 Melt the butter in a large saucepan over a medium heat and add the onion and leeks. Cover and cook, stirring frequently, for 3–4 minutes, until the vegetables begin to soften.

2 Add the stock, rice, carrots, garlic and bay leaf with a large pinch of salt. Bring just to the boil. Reduce the heat, cover and simmer for 25–30 minutes, or until the rice and vegetables are tender. Remove and discard the bay leaf.

3 Add the lettuce to the saucepan and cook, stirring occasionally, for 10 minutes, until the leaves are soft.

4 Remove the saucepan from the heat and leave to cool slightly. Transfer to a food processor or blender, in batches if necessary, and process to a purée.

5 Return the soup to the rinsed-out pan and reheat gently. Stir in the cream, reserving a little for the garnish, and nutmeg to taste. Simmer, stirring occasionally, for 5 minutes, until warmed through.

6 Add the rocket leaves and simmer, stirring occasionally, for 2–3 minutes, until wilted. Taste and adjust the seasoning, adding salt and pepper if needed, and ladle the soup into warmed bowls. Top each serving with a swirl of cream and a few rocket leaves. Serve immediately with crusty bread.

Asparagus Soup

Serves 6

ingredients
- 1 bunch asparagus, about 350 g/12 oz, or 300 g/10½ oz fine asparagus
- 700 ml/1¼ pints vegetable stock
- 55 g/2 oz butter or margarine
- 1 onion, chopped
- 3 tbsp plain flour
- ¼ tsp ground coriander
- 1 tbsp lemon juice
- 450 ml/16 fl oz milk
- 4–6 tbsp double or single cream
- salt and pepper

1 Wash and trim the asparagus, discarding the woody part of the stem. Cut the remainder into short lengths, reserving a few tips for garnish. Fine asparagus does not need to be trimmed.

2 Cook the asparagus tips in the minimum of boiling salted water for 5–10 minutes. Drain and set aside.

3 Put the asparagus stems in a saucepan with the stock, then bring to the boil, cover and simmer for about 20 minutes, until soft. Drain and reserve the stock.

4 Melt the butter in a saucepan. Add the onion and cook over a low heat until soft but only barely coloured. Stir in the flour and cook for 1 minute, then gradually whisk in the reserved stock and bring to the boil.

5 Simmer for 2–3 minutes, until thickened, then stir in the cooked asparagus stems, coriander, lemon juice and salt and pepper to taste. Simmer for 10 minutes. Remove the saucepan from the heat and leave to cool slightly. Transfer to a food processor or blender, in batches if necessary, and process to a purée.

6 Return the soup to the rinsed-out pan, add the milk and reserved asparagus tips and bring to the boil. Simmer for 2 minutes. Stir in the cream and reheat gently. Ladle into warmed bowls and serve immediately.

Mexican Vegetable Soup

Serves 4–6

ingredients

- 2 tbsp vegetable or virgin olive oil
- 1 onion, finely chopped
- 4 garlic cloves, finely chopped
- ¼–½ tsp ground cumin
- 2–3 tsp mild chilli powder
- 1 carrot, sliced
- 1 waxy potato, diced
- 350 g/12 oz diced fresh or canned tomatoes
- 1 courgette, diced
- ¼ small head of cabbage, cored and shredded
- about 1 litre/1¾ pints vegetable stock, chicken stock or water
- 1 fresh corn cob
- about 10 green or runner beans, cut into bite-sized lengths
- salt and pepper
- chopped fresh coriander and sliced fresh green chilli, to garnish
- tortilla chips, to serve

1 Heat the oil in a heavy-based saucepan. Add the onion and garlic and cook for a few minutes, until softened, then sprinkle in the cumin and chilli powder. Stir in the carrot, potato, tomatoes, courgette and cabbage and cook, stirring occasionally, for 2 minutes.

2 Pour in the stock. Cover and cook over a medium heat for 20 minutes, or until the vegetables are tender.

3 Meanwhile, remove and discard the husks and silks from the corn cob, then cut off the kernels using a small sharp knife. Add a little extra stock to the soup if needed, then stir in the sweetcorn kernels and beans and cook for a further 5–10 minutes, or until the beans are tender. Season to taste with salt and pepper.

4 Ladle the soup into warmed bowls and garnish with coriander and chilli. Serve immediately with tortilla chips.

Garden Pea Soup

Serves 4

ingredients
- 600 ml/1 pint vegetable stock
- 450 g/1 lb shelled fresh peas
- pinch of granulated sugar
- 125 ml/4 fl oz single cream, plus extra to serve
- salt and pepper
- crusty bread, to serve

1 Pour the stock into a large saucepan and bring to the boil. Add the peas and cook for 5 minutes.

2 Remove the saucepan from the heat, add the sugar and leave to cool slightly. Transfer to a food processor or blender, in batches if necessary, and process to a purée.

3 Return the soup to the rinsed-out pan, stir in the cream and reheat gently, but do not let it boil.

4 Taste and adjust the seasoning, adding salt and pepper if needed. Ladle into warmed bowls and top each with a swirl of cream. Serve immediately with crusty bread.

Green Vegetable Soup

Serves 6

ingredients
- 3 tbsp olive oil
- 2 leeks, white parts only, chopped
- 2 tbsp plain flour
- 1.5 litres/2¾ pints vegetable stock
- 1 tsp dried thyme
- ½ tsp fennel seeds
- 1 head of Little Gem lettuce, roughly chopped
- 500 g/1 lb 2 oz spinach, coarse stalks removed
- 280 g/10 oz shelled fresh or frozen peas
- 1 bunch of watercress or rocket leaves, about 100 g/3½ oz
- 4 tbsp chopped fresh mint
- salt and pepper
- 2 tbsp chopped fresh flat-leaf parsley, to garnish
- garlic bread, to serve

1 Heat the oil in a large saucepan. Add the leeks and cook over a low heat, stirring occasionally, for 5 minutes, until softened, then remove the pan from the heat.

2 Stir in the flour until fully incorporated, then gradually stir in the stock, a little at a time. Season to taste with salt and pepper, then add the thyme and fennel seeds.

3 Return the pan to the heat and bring to the boil, stirring constantly. Add the lettuce, spinach, peas, watercress and mint, and bring back to the boil. Boil, stirring constantly, for 3–4 minutes, then reduce the heat, cover and simmer gently for 30 minutes.

4 Remove the soup from the heat and leave to cool slightly. Transfer to a food processor or blender, in batches if necessary, and process to a purée. Return the soup to the rinsed-out pan and reheat gently, stirring occasionally.

5 Ladle the soup into warmed bowls, sprinkle with the parsley and serve immediately with garlic bread.

Soup au Pistou

Serves 4

ingredients
- 1 litre/1¾ pints water
- 1 bouquet garni
- 2 celery sticks, chopped
- 3 baby leeks, chopped
- 4 baby carrots, chopped
- 150 g/5½ oz new potatoes, cut into bite-sized chunks
- 4 tbsp shelled fresh broad beans or peas
- 175 g/6 oz canned cannellini or flageolet beans, drained and rinsed
- 3 heads of pak choi
- 150 g/5½ oz rocket leaves
- pepper

pistou
- 2 large handfuls of fresh basil leaves
- 1 fresh green chilli, deseeded
- 2 garlic cloves
- 4 tbsp olive oil
- 1 tsp freshly grated Parmesan cheese

1 Put the water and bouquet garni into a large saucepan and add the celery, leeks, carrots and potatoes. Bring to the boil, then reduce the heat and simmer for 10 minutes.

2 Stir in the broad beans and cannellini beans and simmer for a further 10 minutes. Stir in the pak choi, rocket and pepper to taste and simmer for a further 2–3 minutes. Remove and discard the bouquet garni.

3 Meanwhile, to make the pistou, put the basil, chilli, garlic and oil into a food processor and pulse to form a thick paste. Stir in the Parmesan.

4 Stir most of the pistou into the soup, then ladle into warmed bowls. Top with the remaining pistou and serve immediately.

Spinach & Ginger Soup

Serves 4

ingredients

- 2 tbsp sunflower oil
- 1 onion, chopped
- 2 garlic cloves, finely chopped
- 2 tsp finely chopped fresh ginger
- 250 g/9 oz baby spinach leaves
- 1 small lemon grass stalk, finely chopped
- 1 litre/1¾ pints chicken or vegetable stock
- 225 g/8 oz potatoes, chopped
- 1 tbsp rice wine or dry sherry
- salt and pepper
- 1 tsp sesame oil, for drizzling

1 Heat the sunflower oil in a large saucepan. Add the onion, garlic and ginger, and fry gently for 3–4 minutes, until softened but not browned.

2 Reserve eight small spinach leaves. Add the remaining leaves and the lemon grass to the saucepan, stirring until the spinach is wilted. Add the stock and potatoes to the pan and bring to the boil. Reduce the heat, cover and simmer for about 10 minutes.

3 Remove the saucepan from the heat and leave to cool slightly. Transfer to a food processor or blender, in batches if necessary, and process to a purée.

4 Return the soup to the rinsed-out pan, stir in the rice wine and reheat gently. Taste and adjust the seasoning, adding salt and pepper if needed.

5 Ladle into warmed bowls and top each with a drizzle of sesame oil. Garnish with the reserved spinach leaves and serve immediately.

Corn Chowder

Serves 6

ingredients

- 150 g/5½ oz unsmoked streaky bacon, sliced into small pieces
- 25 g/1 oz butter
- 1 large onion, chopped
- 1 bay leaf
- 5 fresh corn cobs (or 625 g/ 1 lb 6 oz sweetcorn kernels)
- 500 ml/18 fl oz milk
- 2 large garlic cloves, finely chopped
- 2 floury potatoes, cut into small chunks
- 500 ml/18 fl oz chicken stock, preferably home-made
- pinch of cayenne pepper
- 100 ml/3½ fl oz double cream
- salt and pepper
- 3 tbsp chopped fresh coriander or flat-leaf parsley, to garnish

1 Fry the bacon in a large heavy-based saucepan for 5 minutes, or until starting to crisp. Add the butter and, once foaming, stir in the onion and bay leaf. Cover and cook over a medium heat for 7–8 minutes, until the onion is soft but not coloured.

2 Meanwhile, remove and discard the husks and silks from the corn cobs, then cut off the kernels using a small sharp knife. Put about two thirds of the kernels in a blender or food processor with the milk and purée for at least 2 minutes, until smooth. Push through a fine sieve, discarding the solids left in the sieve and reserving the liquid.

3 Add the garlic and potatoes to the pan and moisten with a little of the stock. Add the cayenne pepper and salt and pepper to taste. Cover and cook for a further 5 minutes.

4 Pour the remaining stock and the reserved sweetcorn liquid into the pan and bring to the boil. Reduce the heat and simmer, partially covered, for 5 minutes.

5 Add the remaining sweetcorn kernels and cook for a further 5 minutes. Stir in the cream and adjust the seasoning, adding salt and pepper if needed. Ladle into warmed bowls, garnish with the coriander and serve immediately.

Gazpacho

Serves 4

ingredients

- 250 g/9 oz white bread slices, crusts removed
- 700 g/1 lb 9 oz tomatoes, peeled and chopped
- 3 garlic cloves, roughly chopped
- 2 red peppers, deseeded and roughly chopped
- 1 cucumber, peeled, deseeded and chopped
- 5 tbsp extra virgin olive oil
- 5 tbsp red wine vinegar
- 1 tbsp tomato purée
- about 850 ml/1½ pints water
- salt and pepper
- 4 ice cubes, to serve

1 Tear the bread into pieces and place in a blender or food processor. Process briefly to make breadcrumbs and transfer to a large bowl. Add the tomatoes, garlic, peppers, cucumber, oil, vinegar and tomato purée. Mix well.

2 Working in batches, place the tomato mixture with about the same amount of the measured water in the food processor or blender and process to a purée. Transfer to another bowl. When all the tomato mixture and water have been blended together, stir well and season to taste with salt and pepper. Cover with clingfilm and chill in the refrigerator for at least 2 hours, but no longer than 12 hours.

3 When ready to serve, pour the soup into chilled bowls and float an ice cube in each bowl. Serve immediately.

Chilled Broad Bean Soup

Serves 6

ingredients
- 850 ml/1½ pints vegetable stock
- 650 g/1 lb 7 oz shelled fresh young broad beans
- 3 tbsp lemon juice
- 2 tbsp chopped fresh summer savoury
- salt and pepper
- 6 tbsp Greek-style yogurt, to serve
- chopped fresh mint, to garnish

1 Pour the stock into a saucepan and bring to the boil. Reduce the heat to a simmer, add the broad beans and cook for about 7 minutes, until just tender.

2 Remove the pan from the heat and leave to cool slightly. Ladle into a food processor or blender, in batches if necessary, and process to a purée. Push the mixture through a sieve into a bowl.

3 Stir in the lemon juice and summer savoury and season to taste with salt and pepper. Leave to cool completely, then cover with clingfilm and chill in the refrigerator for at least 3 hours.

4 To serve, stir the soup, taste and adjust the seasoning, adding salt and pepper if needed. Ladle into chilled bowls, top each with a tablespoon of yogurt and garnish with mint. Serve immediately.

Chilled Avocado Soup

Serves 4

ingredients
- 1 tbsp lemon juice
- 2 avocados
- 1 tbsp snipped fresh chives, plus extra to garnish
- 1 tbsp chopped fresh flat-leaf parsley
- 425 ml/15 fl oz cold chicken stock
- 300 ml/10 fl oz single cream, plus extra to serve
- dash of Worcestershire sauce
- salt and pepper

1 Put the lemon juice into a blender or food processor. Halve the avocados and remove the stones. Scoop out the flesh and chop roughly.

2 Place the avocado flesh, chives, parsley, stock, cream and Worcestershire sauce in the blender and process to a smooth purée.

3 Transfer to a bowl and season to taste with salt and pepper. Cover with clingfilm and chill in the refrigerator for at least 30 minutes.

4 To serve, stir the soup and ladle into chilled bowls. Top each with a swirl of cream, garnish with chives and serve immediately.

Chapter 2
Winter Vegetable Soups

Leek & Potato Soup

Serves 4–6

ingredients

- 55 g/2 oz butter
- 1 onion, chopped
- 3 leeks, sliced
- 225 g/8 oz potatoes, cut into 2-cm/¾-inch cubes
- 850 ml/1½ pints vegetable stock
- salt and pepper
- 150 ml/5 fl oz single cream, to serve
- 2 tbsp snipped fresh chives, to garnish

1 Melt the butter in a large saucepan over a medium heat, add the prepared vegetables and sauté gently for 2–3 minutes, until soft but not brown. Pour in the stock and bring to the boil, then reduce the heat and simmer, covered, for 15 minutes.

2 Remove the soup from the heat and leave to cool slightly. Transfer to a food processor or blender, in batches if necessary, and process to a purée. Return the soup to the rinsed-out pan and reheat gently.

3 Taste and adjust the seasoning, adding salt and pepper if needed. Ladle into warmed bowls and swirl the cream on top. Garnish with chives and serve immediately.

French Onion Soup

Serves 6

ingredients
- 1 tbsp olive oil
- 25 g/1 oz butter
- 4–5 onions, about 650 g/ 1 lb 7 oz, thinly sliced
- 3 garlic cloves, finely chopped
- 1 tsp sugar
- 1 tsp salt
- 2 tbsp plain flour
- 150 ml/5 fl oz dry white vermouth
- 2 litres/3½ pints vegetable stock
- 3 tbsp brandy
- salt and pepper

cheese croûtes
- 6 slices of French bread
- 1 garlic clove, halved
- 225 g/8 oz Gruyère cheese, grated

1 Heat the oil with the butter in a large saucepan. Add the onions and stir well, then cover and cook over a very low heat, stirring occasionally, for 15 minutes. Uncover the pan and increase the heat to medium. Stir in the chopped garlic, sugar and salt, and cook, stirring frequently, for 30–40 minutes, until the onions are a deep golden brown.

2 Sprinkle the flour over the onions and cook, stirring constantly, for 3 minutes. Stir in the vermouth and cook, stirring constantly, for 2 minutes, until the alcohol has evaporated, then gradually stir in the stock and bring to the boil. Skim off any foam that rises to the surface, then reduce the heat, cover and simmer for 40 minutes.

3 Towards the end of the cooking time, make the cheese croûtes. Preheat the grill and toast the slices of bread on both sides. Rub each slice with the halved garlic clove, then top with the cheese and grill for a few minutes, until melted.

4 Stir the brandy into the soup and remove the pan from the heat. Taste and adjust the seasoning, adding salt and pepper if needed. Ladle into warmed bowls, top each with a cheese croûte and serve immediately.

Jerusalem Artichoke Soup

Serves 6

ingredients

- 1 tbsp lemon juice
- 700 g/1 lb 9 oz Jerusalem artichokes
- 55 g/2 oz butter
- 1 tbsp sunflower oil
- 1 large onion, chopped
- 1.3 litres/2¼ pints vegetable stock
- 175 ml/6 fl oz milk
- 1 tbsp snipped fresh chives
- 100 ml/3½ fl oz double cream
- salt and pepper
- extra virgin olive oil, for drizzling
- croûtons, to serve

1 Fill a bowl with water and stir in the lemon juice. Peel the artichokes and cut into chunks, then immediately drop them into the bowl of acidulated water to prevent discoloration.

2 Heat the butter with the sunflower oil in a large saucepan. Add the onion and cook over a low heat, stirring occasionally, for 5 minutes, until softened. Drain the artichokes, add them to the pan and stir well. Cover and cook, stirring occasionally, for 15 minutes.

3 Pour in the stock and milk, increase the heat to medium and bring to the boil. Reduce the heat, re-cover the pan and simmer for 20 minutes, until the artichokes are soft.

4 Remove the pan from the heat and leave to cool slightly. Add the chives and transfer the soup to a food processor or blender, in batches if necessary, and process to a purée.

5 Return the soup to the rinsed-out pan, stir in the cream and season to taste with salt and pepper. Reheat gently, stirring occasionally, but do not let it boil. Ladle into warmed bowls, drizzle with extra virgin olive oil and serve immediately with croûtons.

Parsnip Soup with
Ginger & Orange

Serves 6

ingredients

- 2 tsp olive oil
- 1 large onion, chopped
- 1 large leek, sliced
- 2 carrots, thinly sliced
- 800 g/1 lb 12 oz parsnips, sliced
- 4 tbsp grated fresh ginger
- 2–3 garlic cloves, finely chopped
- grated rind of ½ orange
- 1.4 litres/2½ pints water
- 225 ml/8 fl oz orange juice
- salt and pepper
- snipped fresh chives, to garnish

1 Heat the oil in a large saucepan over a medium heat. Add the onion and leek and cook, stirring occasionally, for about 5 minutes, until softened.

2 Add the carrots, parsnips, ginger, garlic, orange rind, water and a large pinch of salt. Reduce the heat, cover and simmer, stirring occasionally, for about 40 minutes, until the vegetables are very soft.

3 Remove the soup from the heat and leave to cool slightly. Transfer to a food processor or blender, in batches if necessary, and process to a purée.

4 Return the soup to the rinsed-out pan and stir in the orange juice. Add a little water if you prefer a thinner consistency. Taste and adjust the seasoning, adding salt and pepper if needed. Simmer for about 10 minutes to heat through.

5 Ladle into warmed bowls, garnish with chives and serve immediately.

Broccoli & Stilton Soup

Serves 6

ingredients
- 40 g/1½ oz butter
- 2 white onions, chopped
- 1 large potato, chopped
- 750 g/1 lb 10 oz broccoli, cut into small florets
- 1.5 litres/2¾ pints vegetable stock
- 150 g/5½ oz Stilton cheese, diced
- pinch of ground mace
- salt and pepper
- croûtons, to serve

1 Melt the butter in a large saucepan. Add the onions and potato and stir well. Cover and cook over a low heat for 7 minutes. Add the broccoli and stir well, then re-cover the pan and cook for a further 5 minutes.

2 Increase the heat to medium, pour in the stock and bring to the boil. Reduce the heat and season to taste with salt and pepper, then re-cover and simmer for 15–20 minutes, until the vegetables are tender.

3 Remove the pan from the heat, strain into a bowl, reserving the vegetables, and leave to cool slightly. Put the vegetables into a food processor or blender, add a ladleful of the liquid and process to a smooth purée. With the motor running, gradually add the remaining liquid.

4 Return the soup to the rinsed-out pan and reheat gently, but do not let it boil. Remove from the heat, add the cheese and stir in until melted and thoroughly combined. Stir in the mace, taste and adjust the seasoning, adding salt and pepper if needed.

5 Ladle into warmed bowls, sprinkle with croûtons and serve immediately.

Winter Vegetable Soup

Serves 6

ingredients

- 2 tbsp vegetable oil
- 1 large onion, thickly sliced
- 1 large potato, cut into chunks
- 3 celery sticks, thickly sliced
- 4 carrots, sliced
- 175 g/6 oz swede, cut into chunks
- 4 large garlic cloves, peeled and left whole
- 1.5 litres/2¾ pints chicken or vegetable stock
- 225 g/8 oz canned chopped tomatoes
- 1 leek, halved lengthways and thickly sliced
- salt and pepper
- 2 tbsp chopped fresh flat-leaf parsley, to garnish
- grated Cheddar cheese, to serve

1 Heat the oil in a large heavy-based saucepan over a medium heat. Add the onion, potato, celery, carrots, swede and garlic cloves. Season to taste with salt and pepper, then cover and cook over a medium heat, stirring occasionally, for 10 minutes.

2 Pour in the stock and tomatoes and bring to the boil. Reduce the heat and simmer, partially covered, for 30 minutes. Add the leek and cook for a further 5 minutes, until just tender.

3 Taste and adjust the seasoning, adding salt and pepper if needed. Ladle into warmed bowls, garnish with the parsley and serve immediately with grated Cheddar cheese.

Sweet Potato & Apple Soup

Serves 6

ingredients

- 15 g/½ oz butter
- 3 leeks, thinly sliced
- 1 large carrot, thinly sliced
- 600 g/1 lb 5 oz sweet potatoes, diced
- 2 large cooking apples, peeled and diced
- 1.2 litres/2 pints water
- freshly grated nutmeg
- 225 ml/8 fl oz apple juice
- 225 ml/8 fl oz single cream
- salt and pepper
- chopped fresh coriander, to garnish

1 Melt the butter in a large saucepan over a low–medium heat. Add the leeks, cover and cook, stirring frequently, for 6–8 minutes, or until soft.

2 Add the carrot, sweet potatoes, apples and water. Season lightly with salt, pepper and nutmeg. Bring to the boil, then reduce the heat, cover and simmer, stirring occasionally, for about 20 minutes, until the vegetables are very tender.

3 Remove the soup from the heat and leave to cool slightly. Transfer to a food processor or blender, in batches if necessary, and process to a purée.

4 Return the soup to the rinsed-out pan and stir in the apple juice. Place over a low heat and simmer for about 10 minutes, until heated through.

5 Stir in the cream and simmer, stirring frequently, for about 5 minutes, until heated through. Taste and adjust the seasoning, adding salt, pepper and nutmeg if needed.

6 Ladle the soup into warmed bowls, garnish with coriander and serve immediately.

Cauliflower Soup

Serves 6

ingredients
- 1 tbsp olive oil
- 25 g/1 oz butter
- 1 large onion, roughly chopped
- 2 leeks, sliced
- 1 large head of cauliflower
- 850 ml/1½ pints vegetable stock
- salt and pepper
- extra virgin olive oil, for drizzling
- finely grated Cheddar cheese, to serve

1 Heat the olive oil and butter in a large saucepan and cook the onion and leeks, stirring frequently, for 10 minutes, taking care not to allow the vegetables to colour.

2 Cut the cauliflower into florets and cut the stalk into small pieces. Add to the pan and sauté with the other vegetables for 2–3 minutes.

3 Add the stock and bring to the boil, then cover and simmer over a medium heat for 20 minutes.

4 Remove the soup from the heat and leave to cool slightly. Transfer to a food processor or blender, in batches if necessary, and process to a purée. Return the soup to the rinsed-out pan and reheat gently.

5 Taste and adjust the seasoning, adding salt and pepper if needed. Ladle into warmed bowls and top each with a drizzle of extra virgin olive oil and a spoonful of grated Cheddar cheese. Serve immediately.

Creamy Mushroom &
Tarragon Soup

Serves 4–6

ingredients

- 50 g/1¾ oz butter
- 1 onion, chopped
- 700 g/1 lb 9 oz button mushrooms, roughly chopped
- 850 ml/1½ pints vegetable stock
- 3 tbsp chopped fresh tarragon, plus extra to garnish
- 150 ml/5 fl oz crème fraîche
- salt and pepper

1 Melt half the butter in a large saucepan. Add the onion and cook gently for 10 minutes, until soft. Add the remaining butter and the mushrooms and cook for 5 minutes, or until the mushrooms are browned.

2 Stir in the stock and tarragon. Bring to the boil, then reduce the heat and simmer gently for 20 minutes.

3 Remove the soup from the heat and leave to cool slightly. Transfer to a food processor or blender, in batches if necessary, and process to a purée.

4 Return the soup to the rinsed-out pan and stir in the crème fraîche. Season to taste with salt and pepper. Reheat gently until warmed through. Ladle into warmed bowls and garnish with tarragon. Serve immediately.

Roasted Pumpkin, Garlic & Thyme Soup

Serves 6

ingredients

- 2 whole garlic bulbs
- 4 tbsp olive oil, plus extra for drizzling
- 900 g/2 lb pumpkin or butternut squash
- 2 tbsp fresh thyme leaves, plus extra sprigs to garnish
- 25 g/1 oz butter
- 1 large onion, finely chopped
- 1 tbsp plain flour
- 1.2 litres/2 pints chicken stock
- 100 g/3½ oz crème fraîche
- salt and pepper

1 Preheat the oven to 190°C/375°F/Gas Mark 5. Take two pieces of aluminium foil, each large enough to wrap a garlic bulb, and place a bulb in the centre of each. Pour ½ tablespoon of the oil over each and sprinkle with salt and pepper to taste, then wrap and place in a large roasting tin. Peel and deseed the pumpkin, then cut the flesh into large chunks. Toss the pumpkin in the remaining oil and sprinkle with salt and pepper to taste and half the thyme leaves. Place in the roasting tin in a single layer and cook in the preheated oven for 1 hour.

2 Melt the butter in a large heavy-based saucepan. Add the onion and cook over a medium heat, stirring occasionally, for 5 minutes, until soft. Stir in the flour and cook for 2 minutes. Add the stock, a few spoonfuls at a time to begin with, then add all the remainder.

3 When the pumpkin has browned, remove the roasting tin from the oven. Add the pumpkin to the pan and simmer for 10 minutes.

4 Open the garlic packages and leave to cool. When cool enough to handle, break up the garlic bulbs, place the cloves on a chopping board and press down on each until the garlic pulp squeezes out.

5 Remove the soup from the heat and leave to cool slightly. Stir in the garlic pulp and the remaining thyme leaves, then transfer to a food processor or blender, in batches if necessary, and process to a purée. Return the soup to the rinsed-out pan and reheat gently.

6 Ladle into warmed bowls and top each with a spoonful of the crème fraîche. Drizzle over a little oil, garnish with thyme sprigs and serve immediately.

Celery & Stilton Soup

Serves 4

ingredients

- 25 g/1 oz butter
- 1 onion, finely chopped
- 4 large celery sticks, finely chopped
- 1 large carrot, finely chopped
- 1 litre/1¾ pints chicken or vegetable stock
- 3–4 fresh thyme sprigs
- 1 bay leaf
- 125 ml/4 fl oz double cream
- 150 g/5½ oz Stilton cheese, crumbled
- freshly grated nutmeg
- salt and pepper
- celery leaves, to garnish

1 Melt the butter in a large saucepan over a low–medium heat. Add the onion and cook, stirring frequently, for 3–4 minutes, until just softened. Add the celery and carrot and continue cooking for 3 minutes. Season lightly with salt and pepper.

2 Add the stock, thyme and bay leaf, and bring to the boil. Reduce the heat, cover and simmer gently, stirring occasionally, for about 25 minutes, until the vegetables are very tender.

3 Remove the soup from the heat and leave to cool slightly. Remove and discard the thyme and bay leaf. Transfer the soup to a food processor or blender, in batches if necessary, and process to a purée.

4 Return the soup to the rinsed-out pan and stir in the cream. Simmer over a low heat for 5 minutes.

5 Gradually add the Stilton to the soup, stirring constantly, until smooth. Do not let it boil. Taste and adjust the seasoning, adding salt if needed and plenty of pepper and nutmeg.

6 Ladle into warmed bowls, garnish with celery leaves and serve immediately.

Potato & Pesto Soup

Serves 4

ingredients

- 2 tbsp olive oil
- 3 rashers rindless smoked bacon, finely chopped
- 25 g/1 oz butter
- 450 g/1 lb floury potatoes, chopped
- 450 g/1 lb onions, finely chopped
- 600 ml/1 pint chicken stock
- 600 ml/1 pint milk
- 100 g/3½ oz dried conchigliette
- 150 ml/5 fl oz double cream
- 2 tbsp chopped fresh parsley
- salt and pepper
- freshly grated Parmesan cheese, to serve

pesto

- 55 g/2 oz finely chopped fresh parsley
- 2 garlic cloves, crushed
- 55 g/2 oz pine kernels, crushed
- 2 tbsp chopped fresh basil leaves
- 55 g/2 oz freshly grated Parmesan cheese
- 150 ml/5 fl oz olive oil
- white pepper, to taste

1 To make the pesto, put all of the ingredients in a food processor or blender and process for 2 minutes, or blend by hand using a pestle and mortar. Scrape into a small bowl and set aside.

2 Heat the oil in a large saucepan and cook the bacon over a medium heat for 4 minutes. Add the butter, potatoes and onions and cook, stirring constantly, for 12 minutes.

3 Add the stock and milk to the saucepan, bring to the boil and simmer for 10 minutes. Add the pasta and simmer for a further 3–4 minutes.

4 Stir in the cream and simmer for 5 minutes. Add the parsley, salt and pepper to taste and 2 tablespoons of the pesto. Ladle the soup into warmed bowls and serve immediately with Parmesan cheese.

Chestnut & Pancetta Soup

Serves 4–6

ingredients

- 3 tbsp olive oil
- 175 g/6 oz pancetta, cut into strips
- 2 onions, finely chopped
- 2 carrots, finely chopped
- 2 celery sticks, finely chopped
- 350 g/12 oz dried chestnuts, soaked overnight
- 2 garlic cloves, finely chopped
- 1 tbsp finely chopped fresh rosemary
- 1 litre/1¾ pints chicken stock
- salt and pepper
- extra virgin olive oil, for drizzling

1 Heat the olive oil in a large saucepan, add the pancetta and cook over a medium heat, stirring frequently, for 2–3 minutes, until starting to brown.

2 Add the onions, carrots and celery and cook, stirring frequently, for 10 minutes, or until slightly golden and softened.

3 Drain the chestnuts, add to the saucepan with the garlic and rosemary, and stir well. Pour in the stock, bring to a simmer and cook, uncovered, for 30–35 minutes, until the chestnuts are beginning to soften and break down – this thickens the soup.

4 Season to taste with salt and pepper. Ladle the soup into warmed bowls, drizzle with extra virgin olive oil and serve immediately.

Mushroom & Sherry Soup

Serves 4

ingredients
- 55 g/2 oz butter
- 2 garlic cloves, chopped
- 3 onions, sliced
- 450 g/1 lb mixed white and chestnut mushrooms, sliced
- 100 g/3½ oz fresh ceps or porcini mushrooms, sliced
- 3 tbsp chopped fresh parsley, plus extra to garnish
- 500 ml/18 fl oz vegetable stock
- 3 tbsp plain flour
- 125 ml/4 fl oz milk
- 2 tbsp sherry
- 125 ml/4 fl oz soured cream
- salt and pepper

1 Melt the butter in a large saucepan over a low heat. Add the garlic and onions and cook, stirring, for 3 minutes, until slightly softened. Add the mushrooms and cook, stirring, for a further 5 minutes.

2 Add the parsley, pour in the stock and season to taste with salt and pepper. Bring to the boil, then reduce the heat, cover and simmer for 20 minutes.

3 Put the flour into a bowl, mix in enough of the milk to make a smooth paste, then stir it into the soup. Cook, stirring, for 5 minutes. Stir in the remaining milk and the sherry and cook for a further 5 minutes. Remove from the heat and stir in the soured cream. Return the pan to the heat and warm gently.

4 Remove from the heat and ladle the soup into warmed bowls. Garnish with parsley and serve immediately.

Curried Vegetable Soup

Serves 4

ingredients
- 40 g/1½ oz butter
- 2 onions, chopped
- 2 garlic cloves, finely chopped
- 1½ tsp ground cumin
- 1 tsp ground coriander
- 1 sweet potato, chopped
- 2 carrots, chopped
- 3 parsnips, chopped
- 1 tbsp curry paste
- 700 ml/1¼ pints vegetable stock
- 700 ml/1¼ pints milk
- 1 tsp lime juice
- 6 tbsp soured cream
- salt and pepper
- naan bread, to serve

fried ginger garnish
- 10-cm/4-inch piece fresh ginger
- 2 tbsp groundnut oil

1 Melt the butter in a large saucepan. Add the onions and garlic and cook over a low heat, stirring occasionally, for 8–10 minutes, until lightly browned. Stir in the cumin and coriander, and cook, stirring constantly, for 2 minutes. Add the sweet potato, carrots and parsnips, and cook, stirring frequently, for 5 minutes, then stir in the curry paste and mix well. Increase the heat to medium, pour in the stock and bring to the boil, stirring occasionally. Reduce the heat, cover and simmer for 20–25 minutes, until the vegetables are tender.

2 Meanwhile, make the garnish. Cut the ginger into thin julienne strips. Heat the oil in a small frying pan over a high heat. Reduce the heat, add the ginger and cook, stirring and turning constantly, for 1 minute. Remove with a slotted spoon and drain on kitchen paper.

3 Remove the soup from the heat and leave to cool slightly. Transfer to a food processor or blender, in batches if necessary, and process to a purée.

4 Return the soup to the rinsed-out pan and stir in the milk. Cook, stirring occasionally, for 5 minutes. Stir in the lime juice and 3 tablespoons of the soured cream. Season to taste with salt and pepper.

5 Ladle the soup into warmed bowls, add a swirl of the remaining soured cream and garnish with the fried ginger. Serve immediately with naan bread.

Borscht

Serves 4

ingredients
- 5 raw beetroots, about
  1 kg/2 lb 4 oz
- 70 g/2½ oz butter
- 2 onions, thinly sliced
- 3 carrots, thinly sliced
- 3 celery sticks, thinly sliced
- 6 tomatoes, peeled, deseeded
  and chopped
- 1 tbsp red wine vinegar
- 1 tbsp sugar
- 2 garlic cloves, finely chopped
- 1 bouquet garni
- 1.3 litres/2¼ pints
  vegetable stock
- salt and pepper
- soured cream and rye bread,
  to serve
- chopped fresh dill, to garnish

1 Peel and coarsely grate four of the beetroots. Melt the butter in a large saucepan. Add the onions and cook over a low heat, stirring occasionally, for 5 minutes, until softened. Add the grated beetroots, carrots and celery, and cook, stirring occasionally, for a further 5 minutes.

2 Increase the heat to medium and add the tomatoes, vinegar, sugar, garlic and bouquet garni. Season to taste with salt and pepper. Stir well, pour in the stock and bring to the boil. Reduce the heat, cover and simmer for 1¼ hours.

3 Meanwhile, peel and grate the remaining beetroot. Add it and any juices to the pan and simmer for a further 10 minutes. Remove the pan from the heat and leave to stand for 10 minutes.

4 Remove and discard the bouquet garni. Ladle the soup into warmed bowls and top each with a spoonful of soured cream. Garnish with dill and serve immediately with rye bread.

Vegetable Goulash Soup

Serves 6

ingredients

- 2 tbsp olive oil
- 1 large onion, chopped
- 2 garlic cloves, finely chopped
- 3–4 carrots, thinly sliced
- ½ head of Savoy cabbage, cored and shredded
- 1 small red pepper, deseeded and chopped
- 1 tbsp plain flour
- 2 tbsp sweet paprika
- 1 litre/1¾ pints vegetable stock
- 2 potatoes, cut into chunks
- 1–2 tsp sugar (optional)
- salt and pepper

1 Heat the oil in a large saucepan. Add the onion, garlic and carrots and cook over a low heat, stirring occasionally, for 8–10 minutes, until lightly coloured. Add the cabbage and red pepper and cook, stirring frequently, for 3–4 minutes.

2 Sprinkle in the flour and paprika, and cook, stirring constantly, for 1 minute. Gradually stir in the stock, a little at a time. Increase the heat to medium and bring to the boil, stirring constantly. Season to taste with salt, then reduce the heat, cover and simmer for 30 minutes.

3 Add the potatoes and bring back to the boil, then reduce the heat, re-cover the pan and simmer for a further 20–30 minutes, until the potatoes are soft but not falling apart.

4 Taste and adjust the seasoning, adding salt and pepper if needed. Stir in the sugar, if using. Ladle the soup into warmed bowls and serve immediately.

Chapter 3
Beans & Pulses

Tuscan Bean Soup

Serves 6

ingredients
- 300 g/10½ oz canned cannellini beans, drained and rinsed
- 300 g/10½ oz canned borlotti beans, drained and rinsed
- about 600 ml/1 pint chicken or vegetable stock
- 115 g/4 oz dried conchigliette or other soup pasta
- 4 tbsp olive oil
- 2 garlic cloves, very finely chopped
- 3 tbsp chopped fresh flat-leaf parsley
- salt and pepper

1 Place half the cannellini and half the borlotti beans in a food processor or blender with half the stock and process until smooth. Pour into a large heavy-based saucepan and add the remaining beans. Stir in enough of the remaining stock to achieve the desired consistency, then bring to the boil.

2 Add the pasta and return to the boil, then reduce the heat and cook for 15 minutes, or until just tender.

3 Meanwhile, heat 3 tablespoons of the oil in a small frying pan. Add the garlic and cook, stirring constantly, for 2–3 minutes, or until golden. Stir the garlic into the soup with the parsley.

4 Season to taste with salt and pepper and ladle into warmed bowls. Drizzle with the remaining oil and serve immediately.

Ribollita

Serves 6

ingredients

- 400 g/14 oz canned haricot or cannellini beans, drained and rinsed
- 3 tbsp olive oil, plus extra for drizzling
- 1 Spanish onion, chopped
- 1 leek, chopped
- 4 garlic cloves, finely chopped
- 2 carrots, diced
- 2 celery sticks, chopped
- 2 potatoes, diced
- 2 courgettes, diced
- 2 large tomatoes, peeled, deseeded and chopped
- 1 tsp sun-dried tomato paste
- 1 dried chilli, crushed (optional)
- 1.7 litres/3 pints vegetable stock
- 225 g/8 oz cavolo nero, cored and shredded
- 225 g/8 oz Savoy cabbage, cored and shredded
- salt and pepper

croûtes

- 6 slices of ciabatta
- 2 garlic cloves, halved

1 Put half the beans into a food processor or blender and process briefly to a coarse purée. Scrape into a bowl and set aside.

2 Heat the oil in a large saucepan. Add the onion, leek, garlic, carrots and celery and cook over a low heat, stirring occasionally, for 8–10 minutes. Add the potatoes and courgettes and cook, stirring constantly, for 2 minutes.

3 Add the tomatoes, sun-dried tomato paste and dried chilli, if using, and cook, stirring constantly, for 3 minutes, then stir in the bean purée. Cook, stirring constantly, for a further 2 minutes.

4 Pour in the stock and add the cavolo nero and Savoy cabbage. Bring to the boil, reduce the heat and simmer for 2 hours.

5 Towards the end of the cooking time, make the croûtes. Preheat the grill. Rub the bread with the halved garlic cloves and toast on both sides.

6 Stir the remaining beans into the soup and heat through gently for 10 minutes. Season to taste with salt and pepper. Put a croûte in the base of each warmed bowl and ladle the soup over the top. Drizzle with a little oil and serve immediately.

Beans & Greens Soup

Serves 4

ingredients
- 250 g/9 oz dried haricot or cannellini beans, soaked overnight and drained
- 1 tbsp olive oil
- 2 onions, finely chopped
- 4 garlic cloves, finely chopped
- 1 celery stick, thinly sliced
- 2 carrots, halved and thinly sliced
- 1.2 litres/2 pints water
- ¼ tsp dried thyme
- ¼ tsp dried marjoram
- 1 bay leaf
- 125 g/4½ oz leafy greens, such as chard, mustard, spinach and kale, stalks discarded
- salt and pepper

1 Put the beans in a saucepan and add enough cold water to cover by 5 cm/2 inches. Bring to the boil and boil for 10 minutes. Drain and rinse well.

2 Heat the oil in a large saucepan over a medium heat. Add the onions, cover and cook, stirring occasionally, for 3–4 minutes, until the onions are just softened. Add the garlic, celery and carrots, and continue cooking for 2 minutes.

3 Add the water, drained beans, thyme, marjoram and bay leaf. When the mixture begins to bubble, reduce the heat to low. Cover and simmer gently, stirring occasionally, for about 1¼ hours, until the beans are tender; the cooking time will vary depending on the type of bean. Season to taste with salt and pepper.

4 Remove and discard the bay leaf. Remove the soup from the heat and leave to cool slightly. Transfer about 450 ml/16 fl oz of the soup to a food processor or blender and process to a purée, then return to the pan and stir well.

5 A handful at a time, cut the greens crossways into thin ribbons, keeping tender leaves, such as spinach, separate. Add the thicker leaves and cook gently, uncovered, for 10 minutes. Stir in any remaining greens and continue cooking for 5–10 minutes, until all the greens are tender.

6 Taste and adjust the seasoning, adding salt and pepper if needed. Ladle the soup into warmed bowls and serve immediately.

Black Bean Soup

Serves 4

ingredients

- 3 tbsp corn oil
- 1 large onion, chopped
- 2 celery sticks, chopped
- 2 garlic cloves, chopped
- 450 g/1 lb dried black beans or black-eyed beans, soaked overnight and drained
- 2.5 litres/4½ pints vegetable stock
- ¾ tsp cayenne pepper
- 5 tbsp lemon juice
- 2 tbsp red wine vinegar
- 2 tbsp dry sherry
- 4 hard-boiled eggs, roughly chopped
- salt and pepper
- chopped celery leaves, to garnish
- grated Cheddar cheese, to serve

1 Heat the oil in a large saucepan. Add the onion, celery and garlic, and cook over a low heat, stirring occasionally, for 6–8 minutes, until softened.

2 Increase the heat to medium, add the beans, pour in the stock and bring to the boil. Reduce the heat, cover and simmer for 2–2½ hours, until the beans are tender.

3 Remove the soup from the heat and leave to cool slightly. Transfer all or half the soup, depending on the texture you require, to a food processor or blender, in batches if necessary, and process to a purée.

4 Return the soup to the pan and bring just to the boil. If it is very thick, add a little water. Stir in the cayenne pepper, lemon juice, vinegar, sherry and hard-boiled eggs, and season to taste with salt and pepper. Reduce the heat and simmer, stirring constantly, for 10 minutes.

5 Remove the pan from the heat and ladle the soup into warmed bowls. Garnish with celery leaves, sprinkle with grated Cheddar cheese and serve immediately.

White Bean Soup
with Olive Tapenade

Serves 8

ingredients

- 350 g/12 oz dried haricot beans, soaked overnight and drained
- 1 tbsp olive oil
- 1 large onion, finely chopped
- 1 large leek (white part only), thinly sliced
- 3 garlic cloves, finely chopped
- 2 celery sticks, finely chopped
- 2 small carrots, finely chopped
- 1 small fennel bulb, finely chopped
- 2 litres/3½ pints water
- ¼ tsp dried thyme
- ¼ tsp dried marjoram
- salt and pepper

olive tapenade

- 1 garlic clove
- 1 small bunch fresh flat-leaf parsley, stems removed
- 240 g/8½ oz almond-stuffed green olives, drained
- 5 tbsp olive oil

1 Put the beans in a saucepan and add cold water to cover by 5 cm/2 inches. Bring to the boil and boil for 10 minutes. Drain and rinse well.

2 Heat the oil in a large heavy-based saucepan over a medium heat. Add the onion and leek, cover and cook, stirring occasionally, for 3–4 minutes, until just softened. Add the garlic, celery, carrots and fennel, and continue cooking for 2 minutes.

3 Add the water, drained beans and the herbs. When the mixture begins to bubble, reduce the heat to low. Cover and simmer gently, stirring occasionally, for about 1½ hours, until the beans are very tender.

4 Meanwhile, make the tapenade. Put the garlic, parsley and olives in a food processor or blender with the oil. Blend to a purée and scrape into a small serving bowl.

5 Remove the soup from the heat and leave to cool slightly. Transfer the soup to a food processor or blender, in batches if necessary, and process to a purée.

6 Return the soup to the rinsed-out saucepan and thin with a little water, if necessary. Season to taste with salt and pepper, and simmer until heated through. Ladle into warmed bowls, top each with a generous teaspoon of the tapenade and serve immediately.

Mixed Bean Soup
with Gruyère

Serves 4

ingredients

- 1 tbsp extra virgin olive oil
- 3 garlic cloves, finely chopped
- 4 spring onions, sliced, plus extra to garnish
- 200 g/7 oz mushrooms, sliced
- 1 litre/1¾ pints vegetable stock
- 1 large carrot, chopped
- 400 g/14 oz canned mixed beans, drained and rinsed
- 800 g/1 lb 12 oz canned chopped tomatoes
- 1 tbsp chopped fresh thyme
- 1 tbsp chopped fresh oregano
- 175 g/6 oz Gruyère cheese, grated
- 4 tbsp double cream, plus extra to serve
- salt and pepper

1 Heat the oil in a large saucepan over a medium heat. Add the garlic and spring onions and cook, stirring, for 3 minutes, until slightly softened. Add the mushrooms and cook, stirring, for a further 2 minutes.

2 Stir in the stock, then add the carrot, beans, tomatoes and herbs. Season to taste with salt and pepper. Bring to the boil, then reduce the heat and simmer for 30 minutes.

3 Remove the soup from the heat and leave to cool slightly. Transfer to a food processor or blender, in batches if necessary, and process to a purée.

4 Return the soup to the rinsed-out pan and stir in the cheese. Cook for a further 10 minutes, then stir in the cream. Cook for 5 minutes, then remove from the heat. Ladle into warmed bowls, top each with a swirl of cream and garnish with spring onions. Serve immediately.

Tomato & White Bean Soup

Serves 6

ingredients

- 3 tbsp olive oil
- 450 g/1 lb red onions, chopped
- 1 celery stick with leaves, chopped
- 1 red pepper, deseeded and chopped
- 2 garlic cloves, finely chopped
- 1 kg/2 lb 4 oz plum tomatoes, peeled and chopped
- 1.3 litres/2¼ pints vegetable stock
- 2 tbsp tomato purée
- 1 tsp sugar
- 1 tbsp sweet paprika
- 15 g/½ oz butter
- 1 tbsp plain flour
- 400 g/14 oz canned cannellini beans, drained and rinsed
- salt and pepper
- 3 tbsp chopped fresh flat-leaf parsley, to garnish

1 Heat the oil in a large saucepan. Add the onions, celery, red pepper and garlic and cook over a low heat, stirring occasionally, for 5 minutes, until softened.

2 Increase the heat to medium, add the tomatoes and cook, stirring occasionally, for a further 5 minutes, then pour in the stock. Stir in the tomato purée, sugar and sweet paprika and season to taste with salt and pepper. Bring to the boil, reduce the heat and simmer for 15 minutes.

3 Meanwhile, mash the butter and flour to a paste in a small bowl with a fork. Stir the paste, in small pieces at a time, into the soup. Make sure each piece is fully incorporated before adding the next.

4 Add the beans, stir well and simmer for a further 5 minutes, until heated through. Ladle into warmed bowls, sprinkle with the parsley and serve immediately.

Chunky Sweet Potato
& Butter Bean Soup

Serves 4

ingredients

- 2 tbsp olive oil
- 1 onion, chopped
- 2 celery sticks, chopped
- 1 large carrot, roughly chopped
- 1 large or 2 small sweet potatoes, chopped
- 400 g/14 oz canned butter beans or cannellini beans, drained and rinsed
- 1 litre/1¾ pints vegetable stock
- salt and pepper
- chopped fresh coriander, to garnish
- freshly grated Parmesan cheese, to serve

1 Heat the oil in a large saucepan over a medium heat. Add the onion, celery and carrot and cook, stirring frequently, for 8–10 minutes, or until softened. Add the sweet potatoes and beans and cook, stirring, for 1 minute.

2 Add the stock, stir thoroughly and bring to a simmer. Season with a little salt and pepper. Cover, reduce the heat and cook for 25–30 minutes, until all the vegetables are tender.

3 Remove the soup from the heat and leave to cool slightly. Transfer one third of the soup to a blender or food processor and process to a purée. Return to the saucepan and mix in well. Taste and adjust the seasoning, adding salt and pepper if needed. Reheat gently until warmed through.

4 Ladle into warmed bowls and sprinkle over the coriander. Serve immediately with grated Parmesan cheese.

Kidney Bean
& Chorizo Soup

Serves 4

ingredients
- 2 tbsp olive oil
- 2 garlic cloves, chopped
- 2 red onions, chopped
- 1 red pepper, deseeded and chopped
- 2 tbsp cornflour
- 1 litre/1¾ pints vegetable stock
- 450 g/1 lb potatoes, halved and sliced
- 150 g/5½ oz chorizo, sliced
- 2 courgettes, sliced
- 200 g/7 oz canned red kidney beans, drained and rinsed
- 125 ml/4 fl oz double cream
- salt and pepper
- crusty bread, to serve

1 Heat the oil in a large saucepan. Add the garlic and onions and cook over a medium heat, stirring, for 3 minutes, until slightly softened. Add the red pepper and cook, stirring, for a further 3 minutes.

2 In a bowl, mix the cornflour with enough of the stock to make a smooth paste and stir it into the pan. Cook, stirring, for 2 minutes. Stir in the remaining stock, then add the potatoes and season to taste with salt and pepper. Bring to the boil, then reduce the heat and simmer for 25 minutes, until the vegetables are tender.

3 Add the chorizo, courgettes and kidney beans to the pan. Cook for 10 minutes, then stir in the cream and cook for a further 5 minutes. Remove from the heat and ladle into warmed bowls. Serve immediately with crusty bread.

Kidney Bean, Pumpkin
& Tomato Soup

Serves 4–6

ingredients

- 250 g/9 oz dried red kidney beans, soaked overnight and drained
- 1 tbsp olive oil
- 2 onions, finely chopped
- 4 garlic cloves, finely chopped
- 1 celery stick, thinly sliced
- 1 carrot, halved and thinly sliced
- 1.2 litres/2 pints water
- 2 tsp tomato purée
- ⅛ tsp dried thyme
- ⅛ tsp dried oregano
- ⅛ tsp ground cumin
- 1 bay leaf
- 400 g/14 oz canned chopped tomatoes
- 250 g/9 oz pumpkin flesh, diced
- ¼ tsp chilli purée, or to taste
- salt and pepper
- fresh coriander leaves, to garnish

1 Put the beans in a saucepan and add enough cold water to cover by 5 cm/2 inches. Bring to the boil and boil for 10 minutes. Drain and rinse well.

2 Heat the oil in a large saucepan over a medium heat. Add the onions, cover and cook, stirring occasionally, for 3–4 minutes, until just softened. Add the garlic, celery and carrot, and continue cooking for 2 minutes.

3 Add the water, drained beans, tomato purée, thyme, oregano, cumin and bay leaf. When the mixture begins to bubble, reduce the heat to low. Cover and simmer gently, stirring occasionally, for 1 hour.

4 Stir in the tomatoes, pumpkin and chilli purée and continue simmering, stirring occasionally, for a further hour, or until the beans and pumpkin are tender.

5 Season to taste with salt and pepper and stir in a little more chilli purée, if liked. Ladle the soup into bowls, garnish with coriander leaves and serve.

Chickpea Soup

Serves 6

ingredients

- 400 g/14 oz dried chickpeas, soaked overnight and drained
- 2 tbsp olive oil
- 1 onion, finely chopped
- 2 garlic cloves, finely chopped
- 450 g/1 lb Swiss chard, stalks discarded and leaves sliced into ribbons
- 2 fresh rosemary sprigs
- 400 g/14 oz canned chopped tomatoes
- salt and pepper
- ciabatta bread, to serve

1 Put the chickpeas into a large saucepan. Add enough cold water to cover and bring to the boil, skimming off any foam that rises to the surface with a slotted spoon. Reduce the heat and simmer, topping up with water if necessary, for 1–1¼ hours, until tender.

2 Drain the chickpeas, reserving the cooking water. Season the chickpeas well with salt and pepper. Put two thirds in a food processor or blender with some of the reserved cooking water and process until smooth, adding more of the cooking water, if necessary, to give a soup consistency. Return to the saucepan with the remaining whole chickpeas.

3 Heat the oil in a medium saucepan, add the onion and garlic and cook over a medium heat, stirring frequently, for 3–4 minutes, until the onion has softened. Add the Swiss chard and rosemary sprigs and cook, stirring frequently, for 3–4 minutes. Add the tomatoes and cook for a further 5 minutes, or until the tomatoes have broken down to an almost smooth sauce. Remove the rosemary sprigs.

4 Add the Swiss chard and tomato mixture to the chickpea purée and simmer for 2–3 minutes. Taste and adjust the seasoning, adding salt and pepper if needed. Ladle the soup into warmed bowls and serve immediately with ciabatta.

Split Pea & Ham Soup

Serves 6–8

ingredients
- 500 g/1 lb 2 oz split green peas
- 1 tbsp olive oil
- 1 large onion, finely chopped
- 1 large carrot, finely chopped
- 1 celery stick, finely chopped
- 1 litre/1¾ pints chicken or vegetable stock
- 1 litre/1¾ pints water
- 225 g/8 oz lean smoked ham, finely diced
- ¼ tsp dried thyme
- ¼ tsp dried marjoram
- 1 bay leaf
- salt and pepper

1 Rinse the split peas under cold running water. Put in a saucepan and add enough water to cover generously. Bring to the boil and boil for 3 minutes, skimming off any foam that rises to the surface. Drain.

2 Heat the oil in a large saucepan over a medium heat. Add the onion and cook, stirring occasionally, for 3–4 minutes, until just softened.

3 Add the carrot and celery and continue cooking for 2 minutes. Add the drained split peas, pour over the stock and water, and stir to combine.

4 Bring just to the boil and stir the ham into the soup. Add the thyme, marjoram and bay leaf. Reduce the heat, cover and cook gently for 1–1½ hours, until the ingredients are very soft. Remove and discard the bay leaf.

5 Taste and adjust the seasoning, adding salt and pepper if needed. Ladle into warmed bowls and serve immediately.

Spicy Lentil & Carrot Soup

Serves 4

ingredients

- 125 g/4½ oz split red lentils
- 1.2 litres/2 pints vegetable stock
- 350 g/12 oz carrots, sliced
- 2 onions, chopped
- 225 g/8 oz canned chopped tomatoes
- 2 garlic cloves, chopped
- 2 tbsp ghee or oil
- 1 tsp ground cumin
- 1 tsp ground coriander
- 1 fresh green chilli, deseeded and chopped
- ½ tsp ground turmeric
- 1 tbsp lemon juice
- 300 ml/10 fl oz milk
- 2 tbsp chopped fresh coriander
- salt and pepper
- natural yogurt, to serve

1 Place the lentils in a large saucepan, together with 850 ml/1½ pints of the stock, the carrots, onions, tomatoes and garlic. Bring the mixture to the boil, then reduce the heat, cover and simmer for 30 minutes, or until the vegetables and lentils are tender.

2 Meanwhile, heat the ghee in a small saucepan. Add the cumin, ground coriander, chilli and turmeric and fry over a low heat for 1 minute. Remove from the heat and stir in the lemon juice. Season to taste with salt.

3 Remove the soup from the heat and leave to cool slightly. Transfer to a food processor or blender, in batches if necessary, and process to a purée. Return the soup to the rinsed-out pan, add the spice mixture and the remaining stock and simmer over a low heat for 10 minutes.

4 Add the milk, taste and adjust the seasoning, adding salt and pepper if needed. Stir in the chopped coriander and reheat gently. Ladle into warmed bowls, top each with a swirl of yogurt and serve immediately.

Bacon & Lentil Soup

Serves 4

ingredients
- 450 g/1 lb rindless smoked bacon rashers, diced
- 1 onion, chopped
- 2 carrots, sliced
- 2 celery sticks, chopped
- 1 turnip, chopped
- 1 large potato, chopped
- 85 g/3 oz Puy lentils
- 1 bouquet garni
- 1 litre/1¾ pints water or chicken stock
- salt and pepper

1 Heat a large heavy-based saucepan over a medium heat. Add the bacon and cook, stirring, for 4–5 minutes, or until the fat runs. Add the onion, carrots, celery, turnip and potato and cook, stirring frequently, for 5 minutes.

2 Add the lentils and bouquet garni and pour in the water. Bring to the boil, reduce the heat and simmer for 1 hour, or until the lentils are tender.

3 Remove and discard the bouquet garni and season to taste with pepper, and with salt, if needed. Remove from the heat, ladle into warmed bowls and serve immediately.

Squash & Lentil Soup

Serves 6

ingredients

- 3 tbsp olive oil
- 2 large onions, chopped
- 2 garlic cloves, chopped
- 2 tsp ground cumin
- 1 tsp ground cinnamon
- ½ tsp freshly grated nutmeg
- ½ tsp ground ginger
- ½ tsp ground coriander
- 1 kg/2 lb 4 oz pumpkin or butternut squash, deseeded and cut into small chunks
- 350 g/12 oz split red or yellow lentils
- 1.7 litres/3 pints vegetable stock
- 3 tbsp lemon juice
- salt and pepper
- crème fraîche or Greek-style yogurt, to serve

1 Heat the oil in a large saucepan. Add the onions and garlic and cook over a low heat, stirring occasionally, for 5 minutes, until softened. Add the cumin, cinnamon, nutmeg, ginger and coriander and cook, stirring constantly, for 1 minute.

2 Stir in the pumpkin and lentils and cook, stirring constantly, for 2 minutes, then pour in the stock and bring to the boil over a medium heat. Reduce the heat and simmer, stirring occasionally, for 50–60 minutes, until the vegetables are tender.

3 Remove from the heat and leave to cool slightly. Transfer to a food processor or blender, in batches if necessary, and process to a smooth purée.

4 Return the soup to the rinsed-out pan and stir in the lemon juice. Taste and adjust the seasoning, adding salt and pepper if needed. Reheat gently. Ladle into warmed bowls, top each with a swirl of crème fraîche and serve immediately.

Golden Vegetable Soup
with Green Lentils

Serves 6

ingredients

- 1 tbsp olive oil
- 1 onion, finely chopped
- 1 garlic clove, finely chopped
- 1 carrot, halved and thinly sliced
- 450 g/1 lb young green cabbage, cored, quartered and thinly sliced
- 400 g/14 oz canned chopped tomatoes
- ½ tsp dried thyme
- 2 bay leaves
- 1.5 litres/2¾ pints chicken or vegetable stock
- 200 g/7 oz Puy lentils
- 450 ml/16 fl oz water
- salt and pepper
- chopped fresh parsley, to garnish

1 Heat the oil in a large saucepan over a medium heat. Add the onion, garlic and carrot, and cook, stirring frequently, for 3–4 minutes, until the onion starts to soften. Add the cabbage and cook for a further 2 minutes.

2 Add the tomatoes, thyme and one of the bay leaves, then pour in the stock. Bring to the boil, reduce the heat to low and cook gently, partially covered, for about 45 minutes, until the vegetables are tender. Remove and discard the bay leaf.

3 Meanwhile, put the lentils in a separate saucepan with the remaining bay leaf and the water. Bring just to the boil, reduce the heat and simmer for about 25 minutes, until tender. Drain off any remaining water and set aside. Remove and discard the bay leaf.

4 When the vegetable mixture is cooked, remove from the heat and leave to cool slightly. Transfer to a food processor or blender, in batches if necessary, and process to a purée.

5 Return the soup to the rinsed-out saucepan and add the cooked lentils. Taste and adjust the seasoning, adding salt and pepper if needed, and cook for about 10 minutes to heat through. Ladle into warmed bowls, garnish with parsley and serve immediately.

Chapter 4
Meat & Poultry

Beef & Vegetable Soup

Serves 4

ingredients

- 55 g/2 oz pearl barley
- 1.2 litres/2 pints beef stock
- 1 tsp dried mixed herbs
- 225 g/8 oz lean rump or sirloin steak
- 1 large carrot, diced
- 1 leek, shredded
- 1 onion, chopped
- 2 celery sticks, sliced
- salt and pepper
- 2 tbsp chopped fresh parsley, to garnish

1 Place the pearl barley in a large saucepan. Pour over the stock and add the mixed herbs. Bring to the boil, cover and simmer gently over a low heat for 10 minutes, skimming off any foam that rises to the surface.

2 Meanwhile, trim any fat from the beef and cut the meat into thin strips.

3 Add the beef, carrot, leek, onion and celery to the pan. Bring back to the boil, cover and simmer for about 1 hour, or until the pearl barley, beef and vegetables are just tender.

4 Skim away any remaining foam that has risen to the top of the soup. Blot the surface with kitchen paper to remove any fat. Taste and adjust the seasoning, adding salt and pepper if needed.

5 Ladle the soup into warmed bowls, garnish with parsley and serve immediately.

Beef & Cabbage Soup

Serves 6

ingredients

- 2 tbsp vegetable oil
- 1 onion, chopped
- 2 celery sticks, diced
- 2 carrots, diced
- 1 large garlic clove, finely chopped
- 1.5 litres/2¾ pints beef stock
- 1 large potato, cut into small chunks
- 280 g/10 oz cooked salt beef, silverside or brisket, cut into small cubes
- 200 g/7 oz shredded green cabbage
- salt and pepper
- 3 tbsp roughly chopped fresh flat-leaf parsley, to garnish

1 Heat the oil in a large heavy-based saucepan over a medium heat. Add the onion, celery and carrots, then cover and cook, stirring occasionally, for 5–7 minutes. Add the garlic, ¼ teaspoon of pepper and salt to taste, then cook for a further minute.

2 Pour in the stock and bring to the boil. Add the potato and beef, then simmer, partially covered, for 30 minutes.

3 Add the cabbage and bring back to the boil. Reduce the heat and simmer for a further 15 minutes, or until the cabbage is tender.

4 Taste and adjust the seasoning, adding salt and pepper if needed. Ladle into warmed bowls, garnish with the parsley and serve immediately.

Beef Noodle Soup

Serves 6

ingredients

- 15 g/½ oz dried Chinese mushrooms or porcini mushrooms
- 3 tbsp corn oil
- 500 g/1 lb 2 oz lean steak, such as fillet or sirloin, cut into thin strips
- 175 g/6 oz carrots, cut into julienne strips
- 10 spring onions, finely shredded
- 2 garlic cloves, finely chopped
- 2.5-cm/1-inch piece fresh ginger, finely chopped
- 1.7 litres/3 pints beef or vegetable stock
- 4 tbsp dark soy sauce, or to taste
- 1 tbsp hoisin sauce
- 6 tbsp Chinese rice wine or dry sherry
- 140 g/5 oz dried egg noodles
- 140 g/5 oz shredded spinach
- pepper

1 Put the dried mushrooms into a bowl, pour in boiling water to cover and leave to soak for 20 minutes. If using Chinese mushrooms, drain and rinse. If using porcini, drain, reserving the soaking water. Strain the soaking water through a fine sieve into a bowl.

2 Heat the oil in a large saucepan. Add the beef and cook, stirring constantly, until browned all over. Remove with a slotted spoon and drain on kitchen paper.

3 Add the carrots, spring onions, garlic and ginger to the pan and cook, stirring constantly, for 5 minutes. Return the beef to the pan, pour in the stock and add the soy sauce, hoisin sauce and rice wine. Add the mushrooms and porcini soaking water, if using. Season to taste with pepper and bring to the boil over a medium heat, then reduce the heat and simmer for 15 minutes.

4 Add the noodles and spinach to the pan, stir well and simmer for a further 7–8 minutes. Taste and adjust the seasoning, adding pepper and soy sauce if needed. Ladle into warmed bowls and serve immediately.

Consommé

Serves 4–6

ingredients

- 1.4 litres/2½ pints strong beef stock
- 225 g/8 oz fresh extra-lean beef mince
- 2 tomatoes, skinned, deseeded and chopped
- 2 large carrots, chopped
- 1 large onion, chopped
- 2 celery sticks, chopped
- 1 turnip, chopped (optional)
- 1 bouquet garni
- 2–3 egg whites
- shells of 2–4 eggs, crushed
- 1–2 tbsp sherry (optional)
- salt and pepper
- julienne strips of raw carrot, turnip, celery or celeriac, to garnish

1 Put the stock and beef in a saucepan and leave for 1 hour. Add the tomatoes, carrots, onion, celery, turnip (if using), bouquet garni, two of the egg whites, the crushed shells of two of the eggs and plenty of salt and pepper. Bring almost to boiling point, whisking hard all the time with a flat whisk.

2 Cover and simmer for 1 hour, taking care not to allow the layer of froth on top of the soup to break.

3 Pour the soup through a jelly bag or scalded fine cloth into a large heatproof bowl, keeping the froth back until the last, then pour the ingredients through the cloth again into a clean pan. The resulting liquid should be clear.

4 If the soup is not quite clear, return it to the pan with another egg white and the crushed shells of two more eggs. Repeat the whisking process as before and then boil for 10 minutes. Strain again.

5 Add the sherry, if using, to the soup and reheat gently. Place the garnish in warmed bowls and carefully pour in the broth. Serve immediately.

Italian Meatball
& Greens Soup

Serves 4–6

ingredients
- 350 g/12 oz fresh lean beef mince
- 4 tbsp grated onion
- 2 tbsp freshly grated Parmesan cheese, plus extra to serve
- 1 small egg, beaten
- 2 litres/3½ pints chicken stock, preferably home-made
- 40 g/1½ oz dried soup pasta
- 350 g/12 oz Swiss chard or Savoy cabbage, stalks discarded and leaves sliced into ribbons
- salt and pepper

1 Preheat the oven to 230°C/450°F/ Gas Mark 8.

2 Combine the beef, onion, Parmesan, ½ teaspoon of pepper and ¼ teaspoon of salt in a bowl, mixing well with a fork. Stir in the beaten egg. Shape into 24 walnut-sized balls and place on a non-stick baking sheet. Cook in the preheated oven for 5–7 minutes, turning once, until lightly coloured. Remove from the oven and set aside.

3 Bring the stock to the boil in a large saucepan. Add the pasta and meatballs, then simmer briskly for 10 minutes.

4 Meanwhile, steam the chard for 2–3 minutes, until wilted. Tip into a sieve and squeeze out as much liquid as possible, pressing with the back of a wooden spoon. Add the chard to the soup and cook for a further 5 minutes, or until the greens and pasta are tender.

5 Taste and adjust the seasoning, adding salt and pepper if needed. Ladle the soup into warmed bowls and serve immediately with Parmesan.

Sauerkraut &
Sausage Soup

Serves 6

ingredients
- 25 g/1 oz butter
- 1 tbsp plain flour
- 1 tbsp sweet paprika
- 2 litres/3½ pints vegetable stock
- 650 g/1 lb 7 oz sauerkraut, drained
- 500 g/1 lb 2 oz smoked pork sausages, cut into 2.5-cm/1-inch slices
- 150 ml/5 fl oz soured cream, plus extra to serve
- salt and pepper

dumplings
- 85 g/3 oz strong white flour, plus extra for dusting
- pinch of salt
- 1 large egg

1 Melt the butter in a large saucepan over a low heat. Add the flour and paprika and cook, stirring constantly, for 2 minutes, then remove the pan from the heat. Gradually stir in the stock, a little at a time, until fully incorporated and the mixture is smooth.

2 Return the pan to medium heat and bring to the boil, stirring constantly. Add the sauerkraut and sausages and season to taste with salt and pepper. Reduce the heat, cover and simmer for 30 minutes.

3 Meanwhile, make the dumplings. Sift the flour and salt into a bowl. Beat the egg in a separate bowl, then gradually beat in the dry ingredients, a little at a time. Turn out onto a floured surface and knead until smooth. Cover and leave to rest for 15 minutes.

4 Divide the dough into six pieces and roll into sausage shapes. Flour your hands, pinch off pieces of the dough and add to the soup. Re-cover the pan and simmer for a further 5 minutes.

5 Remove the pan from the heat and ladle the soup into warmed bowls. Top each with a spoonful of soured cream and serve immediately.

Oriental Pork Balls
& Greens in Broth

Serves 6

ingredients

- 2 litres/3½ pints chicken stock
- 85 g/3 oz shiitake mushrooms, thinly sliced
- 175 g/6 oz pak choi or other Oriental greens, sliced into thin ribbons
- 6 spring onions, finely sliced
- salt and pepper

pork balls

- 225 g/8 oz fresh lean pork mince
- 25 g/1 oz spinach leaves, finely chopped
- 2 spring onions, finely chopped
- 1 garlic clove, very finely chopped
- pinch of Chinese five-spice powder
- 1 tsp soy sauce

1 To make the pork balls, put the pork, spinach, spring onions and garlic in a bowl. Add the five-spice powder and soy sauce and mix until combined.

2 Shape the pork mixture into 24 balls. Place them in one layer in a steamer that will fit over the top of a saucepan.

3 Bring the stock just to the boil in a saucepan that will accommodate the steamer. Regulate the heat so that the liquid bubbles gently. Add the mushrooms to the stock and place the steamer, covered, on top of the pan. Steam for 10 minutes. Remove the steamer and set aside on a plate.

4 Add the pak choi and spring onions to the pan and cook gently in the stock for 3–4 minutes, or until the leaves are wilted. Taste and adjust the seasoning, adding salt and pepper if needed.

5 Divide the pork balls evenly among warmed bowls and ladle the soup over them. Serve immediately.

Chorizo & Kale Soup

Serves 6

ingredients

- 3 tbsp olive oil, plus extra for drizzling
- 1 Spanish onion, finely chopped
- 2 garlic cloves, finely chopped
- 900 g/2 lb potatoes, diced
- 1.5 litres/2¾ pints vegetable stock
- 125 g/4½ oz chorizo or other spicy sausage, thinly sliced
- 450 g/1 lb kale or Savoy cabbage, cored and shredded
- salt and pepper

1 Heat 2 tablespoons of the oil in a large saucepan. Add the onion and garlic and cook over a low heat, stirring occasionally, for 5 minutes, until softened. Add the potatoes and cook, stirring constantly, for a further 3 minutes.

2 Increase the heat to medium, pour in the stock and bring to the boil. Reduce the heat, cover and cook for 10 minutes.

3 Meanwhile, heat the remaining oil in a frying pan. Add the chorizo and cook over a low heat, turning occasionally, for a few minutes, until the fat runs. Remove with a slotted spoon and drain on kitchen paper.

4 Remove the pan of soup from the heat and mash the potatoes with a potato masher. Return to the heat, add the kale and bring back to the boil. Reduce the heat and simmer for 5–6 minutes, until tender.

5 Remove the pan from the heat and mash the potatoes again. Stir in the chorizo, season to taste with salt and pepper, and ladle into warmed bowls. Drizzle with a little oil and serve immediately.

Scotch Broth

Serves 6–8

ingredients

- 700 g/1 lb 9 oz neck of lamb
- 1.7 litres/3 pints water
- 55 g/2 oz pearl barley
- 2 onions, chopped
- 1 garlic clove, finely chopped
- 3 small turnips, cut into small dice
- 3 carrots, finely sliced
- 2 celery sticks, sliced
- 2 leeks, sliced
- salt and pepper
- 2 tbsp chopped fresh parsley, to garnish

1 Cut the lamb into small pieces, removing as much fat as possible. Put into a large saucepan and cover with the water. Bring to the boil over a medium heat and skim off any foam that rises to the surface.

2 Add the pearl barley, reduce the heat and cook gently, covered, for 1 hour.

3 Add the prepared vegetables and season well with salt and pepper. Continue to cook for a further hour. Remove from the heat and leave to cool slightly.

4 Remove the meat from the pan using a slotted spoon and strip the meat from the bones. Discard the bones and any fat or gristle. Place the meat back in the saucepan and leave to cool thoroughly, then chill in the refrigerator overnight.

5 Scrape the solidified fat off the surface of the soup. Reheat gently until warmed through, then season to taste with salt and pepper. Ladle into warmed bowls, garnish with parsley and serve immediately.

North African Harira

Serves 6

ingredients

- 2 tbsp olive oil
- 225 g/8 oz boneless lean lamb, cut into cubes
- 1 onion, chopped
- 115 g/4 oz dried chickpeas, soaked overnight and drained
- 1.5 litres/2¾ pints vegetable stock
- 115 g/4 oz split red or yellow lentils
- 2 large tomatoes, peeled, deseeded and diced
- 1 red pepper, deseeded and diced
- 1 tbsp tomato purée
- 1 tsp sugar
- 1 tsp ground cinnamon
- ½ tsp ground turmeric
- ½ tsp ground ginger
- 1 tbsp chopped fresh coriander, plus extra to garnish
- 1 tbsp chopped fresh parsley
- 55 g/2 oz long-grain rice
- salt and pepper

1 Heat the oil in a large saucepan. Add the lamb and cook over a medium heat, stirring frequently, for 8–10 minutes, until lightly browned all over. Reduce the heat, add the onion and cook, stirring frequently, for 5 minutes, until softened.

2 Increase the heat to medium, add the chickpeas, pour in the stock and bring to the boil. Reduce the heat, cover and simmer for 2 hours.

3 Stir in the lentils, tomatoes, red pepper, tomato purée, sugar, cinnamon, turmeric, ginger, coriander and parsley and simmer for 15 minutes. Add the rice and simmer for a further 15 minutes, until the rice is cooked and the lentils are tender.

4 Season to taste with salt and pepper and remove the pan from the heat. Ladle the soup into warmed bowls, sprinkle with coriander and serve immediately.

Cream of Chicken Soup

Serves 4

ingredients

- 40 g/1½ oz butter
- 4 shallots, chopped
- 1 leek, sliced
- 450 g/1 lb skinless, boneless chicken breasts, chopped
- 600 ml/1 pint chicken stock
- 1 tbsp chopped fresh parsley
- 1 tbsp chopped fresh thyme
- 175 ml/6 fl oz double cream
- salt and pepper
- fresh thyme sprigs, to garnish
- crusty bread, to serve

1 Melt the butter in a large saucepan over a medium heat. Add the shallots and cook, stirring, for 3 minutes, until slightly softened. Add the leek and cook, stirring, for a further 5 minutes. Stir in the chicken, stock and herbs, and season to taste with salt and pepper.

2 Bring to the boil, then reduce the heat and simmer for 25 minutes, until the chicken is tender and cooked through.

3 Remove the saucepan from the heat and leave to cool slightly. Transfer to a food processor or blender, in batches if necessary, and process to a purée. Return to the rinsed-out pan and reheat gently.

4 Stir in the cream and cook for a further 2 minutes, then remove from the heat and ladle into warmed bowls. Garnish with thyme sprigs and serve immediately with crusty bread.

Chicken Soup
with Matzo Balls

Serves 4

ingredients
- 2 chicken quarters
- 2.5 litres/4½ pints vegetable stock
- 2 onions, chopped
- 2 celery sticks, chopped
- 2 carrots, chopped
- 2 tomatoes, peeled and chopped
- 2 fresh parsley sprigs
- 55 g/2 oz dried vermicelli
- salt and pepper
- chopped fresh parsley, to garnish

matzo balls
- 55 g/2 oz butter
- ½ onion, grated
- 1 egg
- 1 egg yolk
- 1 tbsp finely chopped fresh parsley
- 1 tbsp water
- 115 g/4 oz matzo crackers, crushed
- salt and pepper

1 First, make the matzo balls. Melt 15 g/½ oz of the butter in a small frying pan. Add the onion and cook over a low heat, stirring occasionally, for 5 minutes, until softened. Remove from the heat and leave to cool.

2 Beat the remaining butter in a bowl until fluffy, then gradually beat in the egg and egg yolk. Add the parsley and the fried onion, season to taste with salt and pepper and mix well, then beat in the water. Mix in the matzo crumbs until thoroughly incorporated. Cover and leave to rest in the refrigerator for 30 minutes.

3 Meanwhile, put the chicken into a large saucepan and pour in the stock. Bring to the boil over a low–medium heat, skimming off any foam that rises to the surface. Simmer for 15 minutes.

4 Add the onions, celery, carrots, tomatoes and parsley sprigs and season to taste with salt and pepper. Reduce the heat, cover and simmer for 50–60 minutes, until the chicken is cooked through and tender. Meanwhile, shape the matzo mixture into 18 balls.

5 Strain the soup into a clean pan, reserving the chicken quarters. Remove and discard the skin and bones and cut the meat into bite-sized pieces. Add the chicken, vermicelli and matzo balls to the pan, cover and simmer gently for 20–30 minutes. Ladle into warmed bowls, garnish with chopped parsley and serve immediately.

Chicken Soup with
Ginger & Coconut Milk

Serves 4

ingredients

- 400 g/14 oz skinless, boneless chicken breasts, cut into strips
- 100 g/3½ oz Thai fragrant rice
- 1 lemon grass stalk, bruised
- 4 garlic cloves, roughly chopped
- 2 fresh green chillies, deseeded and sliced
- 4 kaffir lime leaves, torn
- 2.5-cm/1-inch piece fresh ginger, chopped
- 4 tbsp chopped fresh coriander, plus extra to garnish
- 1.5 litres/2¾ pints vegetable or chicken stock
- 400 ml/14 fl oz canned coconut milk
- 4 spring onions, thinly sliced
- 115 g/4 oz baby corn
- 115 g/4 oz button mushrooms, halved
- salt
- chopped fresh red chilli, to garnish

1 Put the chicken, rice, lemon grass, garlic, green chillies, lime leaves, ginger and coriander into a saucepan, pour in the stock and coconut milk and bring to the boil over a medium heat, stirring occasionally. Reduce the heat, cover and simmer for 1 hour.

2 Remove the pan from the heat and leave to cool slightly. Remove and discard the lemon grass and lime leaves. Ladle the soup into a food processor or blender, in batches if necessary, and process to a purée.

3 Return the soup to the rinsed-out pan, season to taste with salt and add the spring onions, baby corn and mushrooms. Bring back to the boil, then reduce the heat and simmer for 5 minutes.

4 Remove the pan from the heat. Ladle the soup into warmed bowls, garnish with coriander and red chilli and serve immediately.

Chicken & Rice Soup

Serves 4

ingredients
- 1.5 litres/2¾ pints chicken stock
- 2 small carrots, very thinly sliced
- 1 celery stick, finely diced
- 1 baby leek, halved lengthways and thinly sliced
- 115 g/4 oz petit pois, thawed if frozen
- 175 g/6 oz cooked rice
- 150 g/5½ oz cooked chicken, sliced
- 2 tsp chopped fresh tarragon
- 1 tbsp chopped fresh flat-leaf parsley, plus extra sprigs to garnish
- salt and pepper

1 Put the stock in a large saucepan and add the carrots, celery and leek. Bring to the boil, reduce the heat to low and simmer gently, partially covered, for 10 minutes.

2 Stir in the petit pois, rice and chicken and continue cooking for a further 10–15 minutes, or until the vegetables are tender.

3 Add the chopped tarragon and parsley, then taste and adjust the seasoning, adding salt and pepper if needed.

4 Ladle the soup into warmed bowls, garnish with parsley sprigs and serve immediately.

Chicken Noodle Soup

Serves 6

ingredients
- 2 tbsp vegetable oil
- 1 onion, chopped
- 2 celery sticks, diced
- 3 carrots, diced
- 1 fresh thyme sprig
- 1.5 litres/2¾ pints chicken stock
- 400 g/14 oz skinless, boneless chicken breasts, cut into 1-cm/½-inch chunks
- 50 g/1¾ oz dried fine egg noodles, broken into short lengths
- 3 tbsp chopped fresh flat-leaf parsley
- salt and pepper

1 Heat the oil in a large heavy-based saucepan over a medium heat. Add the onion, celery, carrots, thyme sprig and salt and pepper to taste. Cover and cook, stirring occasionally, for 7 minutes.

2 Pour in the stock and bring to the boil. Reduce the heat, then simmer, partially covered, for 15 minutes, until the vegetables are just tender.

3 Add the chicken and noodles. Bring back to the boil, then simmer for 10 minutes, until the chicken is cooked and the noodles are tender.

4 Taste and adjust the seasoning, adding salt and pepper if needed. Ladle into warmed bowls, sprinkle over the parsley and serve immediately.

Mulligatawny Soup

Serves 4–6

ingredients

- 55 g/2 oz butter
- 2 onions, chopped
- 1 small turnip, cut into small dice
- 2 carrots, finely sliced
- 1 eating apple, cored, peeled and chopped
- 2 tbsp mild curry powder
- 1.2 litres/2 pints chicken stock
- juice of ½ lemon
- 175 g/6 oz cooked chicken, cut into small pieces
- 2 tbsp chopped fresh coriander, plus extra to garnish
- salt and pepper
- 55 g/2 oz cooked rice, to serve

1 Melt the butter in a large saucepan over a medium heat, add the onions and sauté gently for 5 minutes, until soft but not brown.

2 Add the turnip, carrots and apple and continue to cook for a further 3–4 minutes.

3 Stir in the curry powder until the vegetables are well coated, then pour in the stock. Bring to the boil, cover and simmer for 45 minutes. Season well with salt and pepper and add the lemon juice.

4 Remove the saucepan from the heat and leave to cool slightly. Transfer to a food processor or blender, in batches if necessary, and process to a purée. Return the soup to the rinsed-out pan, add the chicken and coriander, and reheat gently.

5 Place a spoonful of rice in each serving bowl and pour the soup over the top. Garnish with coriander and serve immediately.

Turkey & Lentil Soup

Serves 4

ingredients
- 1 tbsp olive oil
- 1 garlic clove, chopped
- 1 large onion, chopped
- 200 g/7 oz mushrooms, sliced
- 1 red pepper, deseeded and chopped
- 6 tomatoes, skinned, deseeded and chopped
- 1.2 litres/2 pints chicken stock
- 150 ml/5 fl oz red wine
- 85 g/3 oz cauliflower florets
- 1 carrot, chopped
- 200 g/7 oz split red lentils
- 350 g/12 oz cooked turkey, chopped
- 1 courgette, chopped
- 1 tbsp shredded fresh basil
- salt and pepper
- crusty bread, to serve

1 Heat the oil in a large saucepan. Add the garlic and onion and cook over a medium heat, stirring, for 3 minutes, until slightly softened. Add the mushrooms, red pepper and tomatoes, and cook, stirring, for a further 5 minutes.

2 Pour in the stock and wine, then add the cauliflower, carrot and lentils. Season to taste with salt and pepper. Bring to the boil, then reduce the heat and simmer gently for 25 minutes, until the vegetables are tender and cooked through.

3 Add the turkey and courgette to the pan and cook for 10 minutes. Stir in the basil and cook for a further 5 minutes, then remove from the heat and ladle into warmed bowls. Serve immediately with crusty bread.

Turkey, Leek & Stilton Soup

Serves 4

ingredients

- 55 g/2 oz butter
- 1 large onion, chopped
- 1 leek, sliced
- 325 g/11½ oz cooked turkey, sliced
- 600 ml/1 pint chicken stock
- 150 g/5½ oz Stilton cheese, crumbled
- 150 ml/5 fl oz double cream
- 1 tbsp chopped fresh tarragon, plus extra leaves to garnish
- pepper
- croûtons, to serve

1 Melt the butter in a saucepan over a medium heat. Add the onion and cook, stirring, for 4 minutes, until slightly softened. Add the leek and cook for a further 3 minutes.

2 Add the turkey to the pan and pour in the stock. Bring to the boil, then reduce the heat and simmer gently, stirring occasionally, for about 15 minutes. Remove from the heat and leave to cool slightly.

3 Transfer half of the soup to a food processor or blender and process to a purée. Return the mixture to the pan with the rest of the soup, stir in the Stilton, cream and chopped tarragon and season to taste with pepper. Reheat gently, stirring.

4 Remove from the heat and ladle into warmed bowls. Garnish with tarragon leaves and serve immediately with croûtons.

Oriental Duck Broth

Serves 4

ingredients

- 2 duck leg quarters, skinned
- 1 litre/1¾ pints water
- 600 ml/1 pint chicken stock
- 2.5-cm/1-inch piece fresh ginger, sliced
- 1 large carrot, sliced, and 1 small carrot, cut into thin strips
- 1 onion, sliced
- 1 medium leek, sliced, and 1 small leek, cut into thin strips
- 3 garlic cloves, crushed
- 1 tsp black peppercorns
- 2 tbsp soy sauce, or to taste
- 100 g/3½ oz shiitake mushrooms, thinly sliced
- 25 g/1 oz watercress leaves
- salt and pepper

1 Put the duck in a large saucepan with the water. Bring just to the boil and skim off any foam that rises to the surface. Add the stock, ginger, sliced vegetables, garlic, peppercorns and soy sauce. Reduce the heat and simmer, partially covered, for 1½ hours.

2 Remove the duck from the stock and set aside. When the duck is cool enough to handle, remove the meat from the bones and slice thinly or shred into bite-sized pieces, discarding any fat.

3 Strain the stock and press with the back of a spoon to extract all the liquid. Skim off as much fat as possible. Discard the vegetables and flavouring solids.

4 Bring the stock just to the boil in a clean saucepan and add the strips of carrot and leek, the mushrooms and duck meat. Reduce the heat and cook gently for 5 minutes, or until the carrot is just tender.

5 Stir in the watercress and continue simmering for 1–2 minutes, until wilted. Taste and adjust the seasoning, adding soy sauce if needed. Ladle the soup into warmed bowls and serve immediately.

Chapter 5
Fish & Seafood

Bouillabaisse

Serves 8

ingredients

- 1 kg/2 lb 4 oz selection of at least 4 different firm white fish fillets, such as red mullet, snapper, sea bass, eel or monkfish, scaled and cleaned, but not skinned
- 500 g/1 lb 2 oz mussels, scrubbed and debearded
- 100 ml/3½ fl oz olive oil
- 2 onions, finely chopped
- 1 fennel bulb, finely chopped
- 4 garlic cloves, crushed
- 1.2 kg/2 lb 10 oz canned chopped plum tomatoes
- 1.5 litres/2¾ pints fish stock
- pinch of saffron strands
- grated rind of 1 orange
- 1 bouquet garni
- 500 g/1 lb 2 oz cooked prawns, in their shells
- salt and pepper
- baguette, to serve

rouille

- 30 g/1 oz fresh breadcrumbs soaked in 1 tbsp water
- 3 garlic cloves, roughly chopped
- 1 egg yolk
- 1 fresh red chilli, deseeded and chopped
- ½ tsp salt
- 175 ml/6 fl oz olive oil

1 First, make the rouille. Put all of the ingredients except the olive oil into a food processor and blend to a paste. Keep blending and add the olive oil in a slow stream until the consistency is that of thick mayonnaise. Chill in the refrigerator until needed.

2 Carefully pin-bone the fish, then cut the fillets into bite-sized pieces. Discard any mussels with broken shells and any that refuse to close when tapped. Set aside.

3 Heat the oil in a very large frying pan or wide saucepan with a lid and gently fry the onion and fennel for about 15 minutes, until soft. Add the garlic and fry for 2 minutes, then add the tomatoes and simmer for 2 minutes. Stir in the stock, saffron, orange rind and bouquet garni and bring to the boil. Simmer, uncovered, for 15 minutes.

4 Add the fish pieces, mussels and prawns, and cover the pan. Simmer for a further 5–10 minutes, until the mussels have opened. Discard any that remain closed. Taste and adjust the seasoning, adding salt and pepper if needed.

5 Remove the soup from the heat and ladle into warmed bowls. Serve immediately with the rouille and baguette.

Mediterranean Fish Soup
with Aïoli

Serves 4

ingredients

- 2 kg/4 lb 8 oz mixed white fish, such as gurnard, red mullet, snapper, grouper and haddock, filleted, with bones, heads and trimmings reserved
- 2 tbsp white wine vinegar
- 2 tbsp lemon juice
- 1.7 litres/3 pints vegetable stock
- 2 tsp herbes de Provence
- 2 bay leaves
- 4 egg yolks
- salt
- croûtes, to serve

aïoli

- 4 garlic cloves
- pinch of salt
- 2 egg yolks
- 125 ml/4 fl oz extra virgin olive oil
- 125 ml/4 fl oz sunflower or safflower oil
- 1–2 tbsp lemon juice

1 Cut out and discard the gills of any reserved fish heads. Cut the fish fillets into chunks and set aside. Put the fish bones, heads and trimmings into a saucepan, pour in the vinegar, half the lemon juice and the stock, add the herbes de Provence and bay leaves and bring to the boil. Season to taste with salt, reduce the heat and simmer for 30 minutes.

2 Meanwhile, make the aïoli. Place the garlic and salt into a mortar and pound to a paste with a pestle. Transfer to a bowl, add the egg yolks and whisk briefly with an electric mixer until creamy. Mix together the oils in a jug and, whisking constantly, gradually add them to the egg mixture. When about half the oil has been incorporated, add the remainder in a thin, steady stream, whisking constantly. Stir in lemon juice to thin to the desired consistency. Transfer the aïoli to a sauce boat, cover and set aside.

3 Strain the cooking liquid from the saucepan into a bowl, measure and make up to 1.7 litres/3 pints with water, if necessary. Return to the saucepan, discarding the fish heads, bones and trimmings and the bay leaves.

4 Beat the egg yolks with the remaining lemon juice in a bowl and stir it into the pan. Add the chunks of fish, stir gently to mix and cook over a low heat for 7–8 minutes, until the fish is just cooked through. Do not allow the soup to boil. Remove from the heat and ladle into warmed bowls. Serve immediately with the aïoli and croûtes.

Genoese Fish Soup

Serves 4

ingredients

- 25 g/1 oz butter
- 1 onion, chopped
- 1 garlic clove, finely chopped
- 55 g/2 oz rindless streaky bacon, diced
- 2 celery sticks, chopped
- 400 g/14 oz canned chopped tomatoes
- 150 ml/5 fl oz dry white wine
- 300 ml/10 fl oz fish stock
- 4 fresh basil leaves, torn
- 2 tbsp chopped fresh flat-leaf parsley
- 450 g/1 lb white fish fillets, such as cod or monkfish, skinned and chopped
- 115 g/4 oz cooked peeled prawns
- salt and pepper

1 Melt the butter in a large heavy-based saucepan. Add the onion and garlic, and cook over a low heat, stirring occasionally, for 5 minutes, or until softened.

2 Add the bacon and celery, and cook, stirring frequently, for a further 2 minutes.

3 Add the tomatoes, wine, stock, basil and half the parsley. Season to taste with salt and pepper. Bring to the boil, then reduce the heat and simmer for 10 minutes.

4 Add the fish and cook for 5 minutes, or until it is opaque. Add the prawns and heat through gently for 3 minutes.

5 Ladle into warmed bowls, garnish with the remaining parsley and serve immediately.

Fish & Sweet Potato Soup

Serves 6

ingredients

- 350 g/12 oz white fish fillet, skinned
- 250 g/9 oz sweet potato, diced
- 1 onion, chopped
- 2 carrots, diced
- ½ tsp ground cinnamon
- 1.7 litres/3 pints fish or vegetable stock
- 400 g/14 oz clams, scrubbed
- 150 ml/5 fl oz dry white wine
- 225 ml/8 fl oz single cream
- salt and pepper
- extra virgin olive oil, for drizzling
- chopped fresh parsley, to garnish

1 Put the fish, sweet potato, onion, carrots and cinnamon into a saucepan, pour in 1 litre/1¾ pints of the stock and bring to the boil. Reduce the heat, cover and simmer for 30 minutes.

2 Meanwhile, discard any clams with broken shells and any that refuse to close when tapped. Put them into a separate saucepan, pour in the wine, cover and cook over a high heat, shaking the pan occasionally, for 3–5 minutes, until the clams have opened. Remove the pan from the heat and lift out the clams with a slotted spoon, reserving the cooking liquid. Discard any clams that remain closed and remove the remainder from their shells. Strain the cooking liquid through a fine strainer into a bowl.

3 Remove the pan of fish and vegetables from the heat and leave to cool slightly. Transfer to a food processor or blender, in batches if necessary, and process to a purée.

4 Return the soup to the rinsed-out pan, add the remaining stock and the reserved cooking liquid and bring back to the boil. Reduce the heat and gradually stir in the cream; do not let it boil. Add the clams, season to taste with salt and pepper, and simmer, stirring frequently, for 2 minutes, until heated through. Drizzle with extra virgin olive oil, garnish with parsley and serve immediately.

Miso Fish Soup

Serves 4

ingredients

- 850 ml/1½ pints fish or vegetable stock
- 2.5-cm/1-inch piece fresh ginger, grated
- 1 tbsp mirin or dry sherry
- 1 fresh bird's eye chilli, deseeded and finely sliced
- 1 carrot, thinly sliced
- 55 g/2 oz daikon, cut into thin strips or ½ bunch radishes, sliced
- 1 yellow pepper, deseeded and cut into thin strips
- 85 g/3 oz shiitake mushrooms, sliced if large
- 40 g/1½ oz dried fine egg noodles
- 225 g/8 oz sole fillets, skinned and cut into strips
- 1 tbsp miso paste
- 4 spring onions, shredded

1 Pour the stock into a large saucepan and add the ginger, mirin and chilli. Bring to the boil, then reduce the heat and simmer for 5 minutes.

2 Add the carrot, daikon, yellow pepper, mushrooms and noodles, and simmer for a further 3 minutes.

3 Add the fish strips with the miso paste and continue to cook for 2 minutes, or until the fish is tender. Ladle into warmed bowls, top with the spring onions and serve immediately.

Fish Soup with Grilled
Peppers & Harissa

Serves 4–6

ingredients

- 2 red or orange peppers
- 2–3 tbsp olive oil
- 1 onion, finely chopped
- 2–3 garlic cloves, finely chopped
- 1–2 tsp harissa
- 1 small bunch of fresh flat-leaf parsley, finely chopped
- 850 ml/1½ pints fish stock
- 175 ml/6 fl oz fino sherry or white wine (optional)
- 400 g/14 oz canned chopped tomatoes, drained
- 1 kg/2 lb 4 oz firm-fleshed fish, such as cod, haddock, ling, grouper, sea bass and/or snapper, cut into large chunks (you can add shellfish too, if you like)
- salt and pepper
- 1 small bunch of fresh coriander, roughly chopped, to garnish
- crusty bread, to serve

1 Using tongs, carefully hold the peppers directly over a gas flame, or cook under a preheated high grill or on a barbecue, turning frequently, for 6–8 minutes, or until the skin blisters and turns black. Put the charred peppers in a polythene bag and leave to sweat for 5 minutes, then hold by the stems under cold running water and peel off the skins. Put the peppers on a chopping board, remove the stems and seeds and cut the flesh into thick strips. Set aside.

2 Heat the oil in a deep heavy-based casserole or saucepan, add the onion and garlic, and cook over a medium heat, stirring frequently, for 2–3 minutes, until they begin to colour. Add the harissa and parsley, and pour in the stock.

3 Bring to the boil, then reduce the heat and simmer for 10 minutes to allow the flavours to mingle.

4 Add the sherry, if using, and the tomatoes. Gently stir in the fish and the grilled peppers and bring back to the boil. Reduce the heat, season to taste with salt and pepper, and simmer for about 5 minutes, until the fish is cooked through. Ladle into warmed bowls, garnish with the coriander and serve immediately with crusty bread.

Cullen Skink

Serves 4–6

ingredients
- 500 g/1 lb 2 oz Finnan haddock or undyed smoked haddock
- 1 large onion, chopped
- 4 fresh parsley sprigs, plus extra chopped parsley to garnish
- 1.3 litres/2¼ pints fish or vegetable stock
- 750 g/1 lb 10 oz potatoes, cut into chunks
- 55 g/2 oz butter
- 850 ml/1½ pints milk
- salt and pepper
- crusty bread, to serve

1 Put the fish, onion and parsley sprigs into a large saucepan. Pour in the stock and bring to the boil, skimming off any foam that rises to the surface. Reduce the heat, cover and simmer for 10 minutes, until the flesh flakes easily.

2 Remove the pan from the heat and lift out the fish with a fish slice. Remove and discard the skin and bones and flake the flesh. Strain the stock into a clean pan.

3 Return the stock to the heat, add the potatoes and bring back to the boil. Reduce the heat and simmer for 20–30 minutes, until tender.

4 Remove the pan from the heat. Using a slotted spoon, transfer the potatoes to a bowl, add the butter and mash until smooth.

5 Return the pan to the heat, add the milk and bring to the boil. Whisk in the mashed potatoes, a little at a time, until thoroughly incorporated. Gently stir in the fish and season to taste with salt and pepper. Ladle into warmed bowls, garnish with chopped parsley and serve immediately with crusty bread.

Salmon & Leek Soup

Serves 4

ingredients

- 1 tbsp olive oil
- 1 large onion, finely chopped
- 3 large leeks, including green parts, thinly sliced
- 1 potato, finely diced
- 450 ml/16 fl oz fish stock
- 700 ml/1¼ pints water
- 1 bay leaf
- 300 g/10½ oz skinless salmon fillet, cut into 1-cm/½-inch cubes
- 90 ml/3 fl oz double cream
- lemon juice, to taste (optional)
- salt and pepper
- fresh chervil or flat-leaf parsley sprigs, to garnish

1 Heat the oil in a heavy-based saucepan over a medium heat. Add the onion and leeks, and cook for about 3 minutes, until they begin to soften.

2 Add the potato, stock, water and bay leaf with a large pinch of salt. Bring to the boil, then reduce the heat, cover and cook gently for about 25 minutes, until the vegetables are tender. Remove and discard the bay leaf.

3 Remove the soup from the heat and leave to cool slightly. Transfer half the soup to a food processor or blender and process to a purée. Return the mixture to the pan with the rest of the soup and stir well. Reheat gently.

4 Season the salmon with salt and pepper and add to the soup. Continue cooking, stirring occasionally, for 5 minutes, until the fish is tender and starts to break up. Stir in the cream, taste and adjust the seasoning, adding a little lemon juice, if using. Ladle into warmed bowls, garnish with chervil sprigs and serve immediately.

Salmon Ramen

Serves 4

ingredients

- 1 litre/1¾ pints fish or vegetable stock
- 1 large garlic clove
- ½ tsp light soy sauce
- 4 salmon fillets, about 140 g/5 oz each, skinned
- groundnut or sunflower oil, for brushing
- 140 g/5 oz dried ramen or fine egg noodles
- 100 g/3½ oz baby spinach leaves
- 4 spring onions, chopped

teriyaki glaze

- 2½ tbsp sake
- 2½ tbsp dark soy sauce
- 2 tbsp mirin or sweet sherry
- ½ tbsp soft light brown sugar
- ½ garlic clove, very finely chopped
- 5-mm/¼-inch piece fresh ginger, very finely chopped

to serve

- 100 g/3½ oz fresh beansprouts
- 1 fresh green chilli, deseeded and sliced
- fresh coriander leaves

1 Preheat the grill to high. Put the stock in a saucepan, add the garlic clove and soy sauce and bring to the boil.

2 Mix together the ingredients for the teriyaki glaze and brush one surface of each salmon fillet with the glaze. Lightly brush the grill rack with oil and cook the salmon under the preheated grill for 4 minutes on one side only. The flesh should flake easily and the centre should remain a bright pink. Remove the fish from the grill and set aside.

3 Cook the noodles in a saucepan of boiling water for 5 minutes or according to the packet instructions, until tender.

4 Remove the garlic from the stock, then bring the stock back to the boil. Drop in the spinach leaves and spring onions and cook until the leaves are just wilted. Use a slotted spoon to remove the spinach and spring onions from the pan and divide them among warmed bowls. Divide the noodles among the bowls, then add a salmon fillet to each. Carefully pour the boiling stock into each bowl.

5 Sprinkle with the beansprouts, chilli slices and coriander leaves and serve immediately.

Hot & Sour Prawn Soup

Serves 2

ingredients

- 300 g/10½ oz large raw prawns, peeled and deveined
- 2 tsp vegetable oil
- 2 fresh red chillies, sliced
- 1 garlic clove, sliced
- about 700 ml/1¼ pints fish stock
- 4 thin slices fresh ginger
- 2 lemon grass stalks, bruised
- 5 kaffir lime leaves, shredded
- 2 tsp palm sugar or soft light brown sugar
- 1 tbsp chilli oil
- handful of fresh coriander leaves
- dash of lime juice

1 Dry fry the prawns in a frying pan or wok until they turn pink. Remove and set aside.

2 Heat the vegetable oil in the same pan, add the chillies and garlic and cook for 30 seconds.

3 Add the stock, ginger, lemon grass, lime leaves and sugar, and simmer for 4 minutes. Add the reserved prawns with the chilli oil and coriander and cook for 1–2 minutes.

4 Stir in the lime juice, ladle the soup into warmed bowls and serve immediately.

Laksa

Serves 4

ingredients

- 1 tbsp sunflower oil
- 2–3 garlic cloves, cut into thin slivers
- 1–2 fresh red Thai chillies, deseeded and sliced
- 2 lemon grass stalks, outer leaves removed, chopped
- 2.5-cm/1-inch piece fresh ginger, grated
- 1.2 litres/2 pints fish or vegetable stock
- 350 g/12 oz large raw prawns, peeled and deveined
- 115 g/4 oz shiitake mushrooms, sliced
- 1 large carrot, grated
- 55 g/2 oz dried egg noodles (optional)
- 1–2 tsp Thai fish sauce
- 1 tbsp chopped fresh coriander, plus extra sprigs to garnish

1 Heat the oil in a large saucepan over a medium heat, add the garlic, chillies, lemon grass and ginger, and cook, stirring frequently, for 5 minutes. Add the stock and bring to the boil, then reduce the heat and simmer for 5 minutes.

2 Stir in the prawns, mushrooms and carrot. If using the egg noodles, break into small lengths, add to the saucepan and simmer for a further 5 minutes, or until the prawns have turned pink and the noodles are tender.

3 Stir in the fish sauce and coriander and heat through for a further minute. Ladle into warmed bowls, garnish with coriander sprigs and serve immediately.

Quick Scallop Soup
with Pasta

Serves 6

ingredients
- 500 g/1 lb 2 oz prepared scallops
- 350 ml/12 fl oz milk
- 1.5 litres/2¾ pints fish or vegetable stock
- 250 g/9 oz frozen petits pois
- 175 g/6 oz dried taglialini
- 70 g/2½ oz butter
- 2 spring onions, finely chopped
- 175 ml/6 fl oz dry white wine
- 3 slices of prosciutto, cut into thin strips
- salt and pepper
- chopped fresh parsley, to garnish

1 Slice the scallops in half horizontally and season to taste with salt and pepper.

2 Pour the milk and stock into a saucepan, add a pinch of salt and bring to the boil. Add the petit pois and pasta, bring back to the boil and cook for 8–10 minutes, until the pasta is tender but still firm to the bite.

3 Meanwhile, melt the butter in a frying pan. Add the spring onions and cook over a low heat, stirring occasionally, for 3 minutes. Add the scallops and cook for 45 seconds on each side. Pour in the wine, add the prosciutto and cook for a further 2–3 minutes.

4 Stir the scallop mixture into the soup. Taste and adjust the seasoning, adding salt and pepper if needed. Ladle into warmed bowls, garnish with parsley and serve immediately.

Manhattan Clam Chowder

Serves 6

ingredients

- 1 tsp sunflower oil
- 115 g/4 oz salt pork or unsmoked bacon, diced
- 1 onion, finely chopped
- 2 celery sticks, chopped
- 4 tomatoes, peeled, deseeded and chopped
- 3 potatoes, diced
- pinch of dried thyme
- 3 tbsp chopped fresh parsley
- 150 ml/5 fl oz tomato juice
- 600 ml/1 pint fish or vegetable stock
- 36 carpetshell or other small clams, scrubbed
- 150 ml/5 fl oz dry white wine
- salt and pepper
- crusty bread, to serve

1 Heat the oil in a saucepan. Add the salt pork and cook over a medium heat, stirring frequently, for 6–8 minutes, until golden brown. Remove with a slotted spoon.

2 Add the onion and celery to the pan, reduce the heat to low and cook, stirring occasionally, for 5 minutes, until softened. Increase the heat to medium and add the tomatoes, potatoes, thyme and parsley.

3 Return the pork to the pan, season to taste with salt and pepper, and pour in the tomato juice and stock. Bring to the boil, stirring constantly, then reduce the heat, cover and simmer for 15–20 minutes, until the potatoes are just tender.

4 Meanwhile, discard any clams with broken shells and any that refuse to close when tapped. Put the remainder into a separate saucepan, pour in the wine, cover and cook over a high heat, shaking the pan occasionally, for 4–5 minutes, until the shells have opened.

5 Remove the clams with a slotted spoon and leave to cool slightly. Strain the cooking liquid through a muslin-lined strainer into the soup. Discard any clams that remain closed and remove the remainder from their shells.

6 Add the clams to the soup and heat through, stirring constantly, for 2–3 minutes. Remove from the heat, taste and adjust the seasoning, adding salt and pepper if needed. Ladle into warmed bowls and serve immediately with crusty bread.

New England
Clam Chowder

Serves 4

ingredients
- 900 g/2 lb clams, scrubbed
- 4 bacon rashers, chopped
- 25 g/1 oz butter
- 1 onion, chopped
- 1 tbsp chopped fresh thyme
- 1 large potato, diced
- 300 ml/10 fl oz milk
- 1 bay leaf
- 375 ml/13 fl oz double cream
- 1 tbsp chopped fresh parsley
- salt and pepper

1 Discard any clams with broken shells and any that refuse to close when tapped. Put the remainder into a large saucepan with a splash of water. Cook over a high heat for 3–4 minutes, until they open. Discard any that remain closed. Strain, reserving the cooking liquid. Leave until cool enough to handle.

2 Reserve some clams in their shells for the garnish, then remove the remainder from their shells, chopping them roughly if large, and set aside.

3 In a clean saucepan, dry-fry the bacon until browned and crisp. Drain on kitchen paper. Add the butter to the same saucepan and, when it has melted, add the onion. Cook for 4–5 minutes, until soft but not coloured. Add the thyme and cook briefly before adding the potato, reserved cooking liquid, milk and bay leaf. Bring to the boil, then reduce the heat and leave to simmer for 10 minutes, or until the potato is just tender.

4 Remove the soup from the heat and leave to cool slightly. Remove and discard the bay leaf, then transfer the soup to a food processor or blender, in batches if necessary, and process to a purée.

5 Return the soup to the rinsed-out pan and add the clams, bacon and cream. Simmer for a further 2–3 minutes, until heated through. Season to taste with salt and pepper. Stir in the parsley and ladle the soup into warmed bowls. Garnish with the reserved clams in their shells and serve immediately.

Mussel Soup

Serves 6

ingredients

- 48 mussels, scrubbed and debearded
- 1 onion, finely chopped
- 2 tbsp chopped fresh parsley
- 2 bay leaves
- 250 ml/9 fl oz dry cider
- 55 g/2 oz butter
- 2 celery sticks, chopped
- 2 leeks, thinly sliced
- 600 ml/1 pint milk
- 40 g/1½ oz plain flour
- 600 ml/1 pint fish or vegetable stock
- pinch of freshly grated nutmeg
- ½ tsp fennel seeds
- 225 ml/8 fl oz double cream
- salt and pepper
- wholemeal bread, to serve

1 Discard any mussels with broken shells and any that refuse to close when tapped. Sprinkle the onion, parsley and bay leaves over the base of a large saucepan and put the mussels on top. Season to taste with salt and pepper, then pour in the cider. Cover, bring to the boil over a high heat and cook, shaking the pan occasionally, for 4–5 minutes, until the mussels have opened.

2 Remove the pan from the heat and lift out the mussels. Discard any that remain closed. Remove the remainder from their shells and set aside. Strain the cooking liquid into a bowl.

3 Melt the butter in a separate saucepan. Add the celery and leeks and cook over a low heat, stirring occasionally, for 8 minutes, until lightly browned. Meanwhile, pour the milk into another saucepan and bring just to the boil, then remove from the heat.

4 Sprinkle the flour over the vegetables and cook, stirring constantly, for 2 minutes. Increase the heat and gradually stir in the warm milk, then pour in the stock. Bring to the boil, stirring constantly, then reduce the heat and simmer for 15 minutes.

5 Remove the pan from the heat and strain the soup into a bowl. Return to the rinsed-out pan, add the reserved cooking liquid, the nutmeg, fennel seeds and mussels. Stir in the cream and reheat gently, but do not let it boil. Ladle into warmed bowls and serve immediately with wholemeal bread.

Carrot & Mussel Soup

Serves 4–6

ingredients

- 1 kg/2 lb 4 oz carrots
- 100 g/3½ oz butter
- 1 tsp sugar
- 1.3 litres/2¼ pints fish or vegetable stock
- 48 mussels, scrubbed and debearded
- 300 ml/10 fl oz dry white wine
- 1 garlic clove, roughly chopped
- salt and pepper
- 2 tbsp chopped fresh parsley, to garnish
- wholemeal bread rolls, to serve

1 Reserve three of the carrots and slice the remainder. Melt 55 g/2 oz of the butter in a large saucepan. Add the sliced carrots and half the sugar and cook over a low heat, stirring occasionally, for 5 minutes. Increase the heat to medium, pour in the stock, season to taste with salt and bring to the boil.

2 Reduce the heat, cover and simmer, stirring occasionally, for 25 minutes. Meanwhile, finely chop the reserved carrots. Melt the remaining butter in a small saucepan. Add the chopped carrots and the remaining sugar and cook over a low heat, stirring occasionally, for 10 minutes. Remove from the heat.

3 Discard any mussels with broken shells and any that refuse to close when tapped. Put the remainder into a saucepan, pour in the wine and add the garlic. Cover and cook over a high heat, shaking the pan occasionally, for 4–5 minutes, until the mussels have opened. Remove the pan from the heat and lift out the mussels. Discard any that remain closed. Remove the mussels from their shells. Strain the cooking liquid through a muslin-lined strainer into a bowl.

4 Remove the saucepan of stock and sliced carrots from the heat and leave to cool slightly. Transfer to a food processor or blender, add the cooking liquid and process to a purée. Return the soup to the rinsed-out pan, season to taste with salt and pepper, and reheat gently.

5 Gently stir the mussels into the soup along with the carrot and sugar mixture. Ladle into warmed bowls, garnish with parsley and serve immediately with bread rolls.

Cajun Crab & Sweetcorn Chowder

Serves 6

ingredients
- 40 g/1½ oz butter
- 1 onion, finely chopped
- 2 garlic cloves, finely chopped
- 2 celery sticks, finely chopped
- 1 small carrot, finely chopped
- 175 ml/6 fl oz medium-dry white wine
- 500 ml/18 fl oz fish or vegetable stock
- 250 g/9 oz frozen sweetcorn kernels
- pinch of cayenne pepper
- ½ tsp dried mixed herbs
- 350 ml/12 fl oz double cream
- 175 ml/6 fl oz crème fraîche
- 1 tbsp chopped fresh dill
- 225 g/8 oz white crabmeat
- salt and pepper
- wholemeal bread rolls, to serve

1 Melt the butter in a large saucepan. Add the onion, garlic, celery and carrot, and cook over a low heat, stirring occasionally, for 5 minutes, until softened.

2 Increase the heat to medium, pour in the wine and cook for 2 minutes, until the alcohol has evaporated. Pour in the stock and bring to the boil, then add the sweetcorn, cayenne pepper and mixed herbs. Bring back to the boil, reduce the heat and simmer for 15 minutes.

3 Add the cream and simmer gently over a very low heat for a further 10–15 minutes, but do not let it boil.

4 Gradually add the crème fraîche, whisking constantly with a balloon whisk, then stir in the dill and crabmeat and season to taste with salt and pepper. Heat gently for 3–4 minutes. Ladle into warmed bowls and serve immediately with bread rolls.

Lobster Bisque

Serves 4

ingredients

- 450 g/1 lb cooked lobster
- 40 g/1½ oz butter
- 1 small carrot, grated
- 1 celery stick, finely chopped
- 1 leek, finely chopped
- 1 small onion, finely chopped
- 2 shallots, finely chopped
- 3 tbsp brandy or Cognac
- 50 ml/2 fl oz dry white wine
- 1.2 litres/2 pints water
- 1 tbsp tomato purée
- 125 ml/4 fl oz whipping cream, or to taste
- 6 tbsp plain flour
- 2–3 tbsp water
- salt and pepper
- snipped fresh chives, to garnish

1 Pull off the lobster tail. With the legs up, cut the body in half lengthways. Scoop out the tomalley (the soft pale greenish-grey part) and, if it is a female, the roe (the solid red-orange part). Reserve these together, cover and chill in the refrigerator. Remove the meat and cut into bite-sized pieces, then cover and chill in the refrigerator. Chop the shell into large pieces.

2 Melt half the butter in a large saucepan over a medium heat and add the lobster shell pieces. Fry until brown bits begin to stick on the bottom of the pan. Add the carrot, celery, leek, onion and shallots. Cook, stirring, for 1½–2 minutes (do not allow to burn). Add the brandy and wine and bubble for 1 minute. Pour over the water, add the tomato purée and a large pinch of salt, and bring to the boil. Reduce the heat and simmer for 30 minutes, then strain the stock, discarding the solids.

3 Melt the remaining butter in a small saucepan and add the tomalley and roe, if any. Add the cream and whisk to mix well, then remove from the heat and set aside.

4 Put the flour in a small mixing bowl and very slowly whisk in the cold water. Stir in a little of the hot stock mixture to make a smooth liquid.

5 Bring the remaining lobster stock to the boil and whisk in the flour mixture. Boil gently for 4–5 minutes, or until the soup thickens. Press the tomalley, roe and cream mixture through a sieve into the soup, then add the lobster meat. Simmer until heated through.

6 Taste and adjust the seasoning, adding salt and pepper if needed. Stir in a little more cream if wished. Ladle into warmed bowls, garnish with chives and serve immediately.

Chapter 6
Accompaniments

Croûtons

Serves 4–6

ingredients

- 2 slices day-old white, wholemeal or granary bread, crusts removed
- 4 tbsp vegetable or olive oil
- 1 garlic clove, finely chopped (optional)
- finely chopped fresh herbs, such as parsley and thyme (optional)
- ½ tsp paprika or chilli powder (optional)
- 1 tbsp freshly grated Parmesan cheese (optional)
- salt and pepper

1 Cut the bread into 1-cm/½-inch cubes.

2 Heat the oil in a frying pan and add the garlic, if using, and bread cubes in a single layer, tossing occasionally, until the bread is golden brown and crisp.

3 Remove the pan from the heat and spoon out the croûtons onto kitchen paper to drain.

4 Whilst the croûtons are still hot, toss them in the fresh herbs, paprika or Parmesan, if using. Season to taste with salt and pepper. The croûtons are best used on the day of making.

Seeded Bread Rolls

Makes 8

ingredients
- 450 g/1 lb strong white flour, plus extra for dusting
- 1 tsp salt
- 1½ tsp easy-blend dried yeast
- 1 tbsp vegetable oil, plus extra for brushing
- 350 ml/12 fl oz lukewarm water
- 1 egg, beaten
- sesame or poppy seeds, for sprinkling

1 Place the flour, salt and yeast in a large bowl and mix well. Pour in the oil and add the water, then mix well to make a smooth dough.

2 Turn out onto a lightly floured surface and knead well for 5–7 minutes, until smooth and elastic. Brush a bowl with oil. Shape the dough into a ball, place it in the bowl and cover with a damp tea towel. Leave to rise in a warm place for 1 hour, until the dough has doubled in volume.

3 Turn out the dough onto a lightly floured surface and knead briefly until smooth. Divide the dough into eight pieces. Shape half the dough into round rolls. Make the other half into cottage rolls with a small round shape on top. Place the rolls on a baking sheet.

4 Cover the rolls with a damp tea towel and leave to rise for 30 minutes, until the rolls have doubled in size.

5 Preheat the oven to 220°C/425°F/Gas Mark 7. Brush the rolls with the beaten egg and sprinkle with seeds. Bake in the preheated oven for 10–15 minutes, until golden brown. Test that the rolls are cooked by tapping on the bases with your knuckles – they should sound hollow. Transfer to a wire rack to cool.

Crusty White Bread

Makes 1 loaf

ingredients
- 1 egg
- 1 egg yolk
- lukewarm water, as required
- 500 g/1 lb 2 oz strong white flour, plus extra for dusting
- 1½ tsp salt
- 2 tsp sugar
- 1 tsp easy-blend dried yeast
- 25 g/1 oz butter, diced
- sunflower oil, for greasing

1 Place the egg and egg yolk in a jug and beat lightly to mix. Add enough lukewarm water to make up to 300 ml/ 10 fl oz. Stir well.

2 Place the flour, salt, sugar and yeast in a large bowl. Add the butter and rub it in with your fingertips until the mixture resembles breadcrumbs. Make a well in the centre, add the egg mixture and work to a smooth dough.

3 Turn out onto a lightly floured surface and knead well for about 10 minutes, until smooth. Brush a bowl with oil. Shape the dough into a ball, place it in the bowl and cover with a damp tea towel. Leave to rise in a warm place for 1 hour, until the dough has doubled in volume.

4 Oil a 900-g/2-lb loaf tin. Turn the dough out onto a lightly floured surface and knead for 1 minute, until smooth. Shape the dough the length of the tin and three times the width. Fold the dough into three lengthways and place it in the tin with the join underneath. Cover and leave in a warm place for 30 minutes, until it has risen above the tin.

5 Preheat the oven to 220°C/425°F/ Gas Mark 7. Bake in the preheated oven for 30 minutes, or until firm and golden brown. Test that the loaf is cooked by tapping on the base with your knuckles – it should sound hollow. Transfer to a wire rack to cool.

Wholemeal Harvest Bread

Makes 1 loaf

ingredients

- 225 g/8 oz strong wholemeal flour, plus extra for dusting
- 1 tbsp skimmed milk powder
- 1 tsp salt
- 2 tbsp soft light brown sugar
- 1 tsp easy-blend dried yeast
- 1½ tbsp sunflower oil, plus extra for greasing
- 175 ml/6 fl oz lukewarm water

1 Place the flour, milk powder, salt, sugar and yeast in a large bowl. Pour in the oil and add the water, then mix well to make a smooth dough.

2 Turn out onto a lightly floured surface and knead well for about 10 minutes, until smooth. Brush a bowl with oil. Shape the dough into a ball, place it in the bowl and cover with a damp tea towel. Leave to rise in a warm place for 1 hour, until the dough has doubled in volume.

3 Oil a 900-g/2-lb loaf tin. Turn the dough out onto a lightly floured surface and knead for 1 minute, until smooth. Shape the dough the length of the tin and three times the width. Fold the dough into three lengthways and place it in the tin with the join underneath. Cover and leave in a warm place for 30 minutes, until it has risen above the tin.

4 Preheat the oven to 220°C/425°F/ Gas Mark 7. Bake in the preheated oven for 30 minutes, or until firm and golden brown. Test that the loaf is cooked by tapping on the base with your knuckles – it should sound hollow. Transfer to a wire rack to cool.

Mixed Seed Bread

Makes 1 loaf

ingredients

- 375 g/13 oz strong white flour, plus extra for dusting
- 125 g/4½ oz rye flour
- 1½ tbsp skimmed milk powder
- 1½ tsp salt
- 1 tbsp soft light brown sugar
- 1 tsp easy-blend dried yeast
- 1½ tbsp sunflower oil, plus extra for greasing
- 2 tsp lemon juice
- 300 ml/10 fl oz lukewarm water
- 1 tsp caraway seeds
- ½ tsp poppy seeds
- ½ tsp sesame seeds

topping

- 1 egg white
- 1 tbsp water
- 1 tbsp sunflower seeds or pumpkin seeds

1 Place the flours, milk powder, salt, sugar and yeast in a large bowl. Pour in the oil and add the lemon juice and water. Stir in the seeds and mix well to make a smooth dough. Turn out onto a lightly floured surface and knead well for about 10 minutes, until smooth.

2 Brush a bowl with oil. Shape the dough into a ball, place it in the bowl and cover with a damp tea towel. Leave to rise in a warm place for 1 hour, until the dough has doubled in volume.

3 Oil a 900-g/2-lb loaf tin. Turn out the dough onto a lightly floured surface and knead for 1 minute, until smooth. Shape the dough the length of the tin and three times the width. Fold the dough in three lengthways and place it in the tin with the join underneath. Cover and leave in a warm place for 30 minutes, until it has risen above the tin.

4 Preheat the oven to 220°C/425°F/Gas Mark 7. For the topping, lightly beat the egg white with the water to make a glaze. Just before baking, brush the glaze over the loaf, then gently press the sunflower seeds all over the top.

5 Bake in the preheated oven for 30 minutes, or until firm and golden brown. Test that the loaf is cooked by tapping on the base with your knuckles – it should sound hollow. Transfer to a wire rack to cool.

Rye Bread

Makes 1 loaf

ingredients
- 450 g/1 lb rye flour
- 225 g/8 oz strong white flour, plus extra for dusting
- 2 tsp salt
- 2 tsp soft light brown sugar
- 1½ tsp easy-blend dried yeast
- 425 ml/15 fl oz lukewarm water
- 2 tsp vegetable oil, plus extra for greasing

glaze
- 1 egg white
- 1 tbsp water

1 Sift the flours and salt together into a bowl. Add the sugar and yeast and stir to mix. Make a well in the centre and pour in the water and oil.

2 Stir until the dough begins to come together, then knead until it leaves the side of the bowl. Turn out onto a lightly floured surface and knead for 10 minutes, until elastic and smooth.

3 Brush a bowl with oil. Shape the dough into a ball, put it in the bowl and cover with a damp tea towel. Leave to rise in a warm place for 2 hours, or until doubled in volume.

4 Oil a baking sheet. Turn out the dough onto a lightly floured surface and knock back, then knead for 10 minutes.

5 Shape the dough into a ball, put it on the prepared baking sheet and cover. Leave to rise in a warm place for a further 40 minutes, or until doubled in volume.

6 Preheat the oven to 190°C/375°F/ Gas Mark 5. Lightly beat the egg white with the water to make a glaze.

7 Bake the loaf in the preheated oven for 20 minutes, then remove from the oven and brush the top with half the glaze. Return to the oven and bake for a further 20 minutes.

8 Brush the top of the loaf with the remaining glaze and return to the oven for a further 20–30 minutes, until the crust is a rich brown colour. Test that the loaf is cooked by tapping on the base with your knuckles – it should sound hollow. Transfer to a wire rack to cool.

Irish Soda Bread

Makes 1 loaf

ingredients

- 280 g/10 oz plain white flour, plus extra for dusting
- 280 g/10 oz wholemeal flour
- 1½ tsp bicarbonate of soda
- 1 tsp salt
- 1 tsp dark muscovado sugar
- about 425 ml/15 fl oz buttermilk

1 Preheat the oven to 230°C/450°F/ Gas Mark 8. Dust a baking sheet with flour. Sift the flours, bicarbonate of soda and salt into a bowl and stir in the sugar. Make a well in the centre and pour in enough of the buttermilk to make a dough that is soft but not too wet and sticky. Add a little more buttermilk, if necessary.

2 Turn the dough out onto a floured work surface and knead very briefly into a large round, about 5 cm/2 inches thick. Dust lightly with flour and, using a sharp knife, mark the top of the loaf with a deep cross.

3 Place the loaf on the prepared baking sheet and bake in the preheated oven for 15 minutes. Reduce the oven temperature to 200°C/400°F/Gas Mark 6 and bake for a further 20–25 minutes, or until firm and golden brown. Test that the loaf is cooked by tapping on the base with your knuckles – it should sound hollow. Transfer to a wire rack to cool.

Buttermilk Scones

Serves 4

Makes 6–7

ingredients
- 225 g /8 oz plain flour, plus extra for dusting
- 1 tsp salt
- 1 tsp bicarbonate of soda
- 1 tsp cream of tartar
- ¼ tsp pepper
- 50 g/1¾ oz butter
- 150 ml/5 fl oz buttermilk or soured cream
- beaten egg yolk, to glaze

1 Sift the flour, salt, bicarbonate of soda and cream of tartar into a bowl. Sift again to mix thoroughly. Stir in the pepper.

2 Rub in the butter using your fingertips until the mixture resembles fine breadcrumbs. Make a well in the centre and pour in the buttermilk. Mix with a fork to form a soft dough. Turn out onto a lightly floured surface and knead very gently until the dough is smooth.

3 Roll out the dough to a thickness of 2 cm/¾ inch. Cut into rounds using a 6-cm/2½-inch cutter. Leave to stand for 15 minutes.

4 Preheat the oven to 220°C/425°F/ Gas Mark 7. Put a non-stick baking sheet in the oven to heat. Brush the scones with beaten egg yolk and place on the baking sheet. Bake in the preheated oven for 15 minutes, until browned and well risen. Transfer to a wire rack to cool.

Chilli Cornbread Muffins

Makes 12

ingredients
- 175 g/6 oz plain flour
- 4 tsp baking powder
- 175 g/6 oz cornmeal or polenta
- 2 tbsp caster sugar
- 1 tsp salt
- 4 spring onions, finely chopped
- 1 fresh red chilli, deseeded and finely chopped
- 3 eggs, beaten
- 150 ml/5 fl oz natural yogurt
- 150 ml/5 fl oz milk

1 Preheat the oven to 200°C/400°F/Gas Mark 6. Line a 12-hole muffin tin with paper cases.

2 Sift the flour and baking powder into a large bowl. Stir in the cornmeal, sugar, salt, spring onions and chilli.

3 Beat together the eggs, yogurt and milk, then pour into the flour mixture and beat until just combined. Spoon the mixture into the muffin cases.

4 Bake the muffins in the preheated oven for 15–20 minutes, until risen, golden and just firm to the touch. Transfer to a wire rack to cool.